Job

Insider's Guide to Interviews and Getting the Job You Want

(Speaking Skills and Body Language for Winning Interview)

Michael Rubin

Published by Rob Miles

Michael Rubin

All Rights Reserved

Job: Insider's Guide to Interviews and Getting the Job You Want (Speaking Skills and Body Language for Winning Interview)

ISBN 978-1-989990-67-4

All rights reserved. No part of this guide may be reproduced in any form without permission in writing from the publisher except in the case of brief quotations embodied in critical articles or reviews.

Legal & Disclaimer

The information contained in this book is not designed to replace or take the place of any form of medicine or professional medical advice. The information in this book has been provided for educational and entertainment purposes only.

The information contained in this book has been compiled from sources deemed reliable, and it is accurate to the best of the Author's knowledge; however, the Author cannot guarantee its accuracy and validity and cannot be held liable for any errors or omissions. Changes are periodically made to this book. You must consult your doctor or get professional medical advice before using any of the suggested remedies, techniques, or information in this book.

Upon using the information contained in this book, you agree to hold harmless the Author from and against any damages, costs, and expenses, including any legal fees potentially resulting from the application of any of the information provided by this guide. This disclaimer applies to any damages or injury caused by the use and application, whether directly or indirectly, of any advice or information presented, whether for breach of contract, tort, negligence, personal injury, criminal intent, or under any other cause of action.

You agree to accept all risks of using the information presented inside this book. You need to consult a professional medical practitioner in order to ensure you are both able and healthy enough to participate in this program.

Table of Contents

INTRODUCTION 1

CHAPTER 1: BASIC TIPS FOR A GREAT JOB INTERVIEW 3

CHAPTER 2: SUIT UP! 7

CHAPTER 3: THINGS TO DO BEFORE A JOB INTERVIEW.... 11

CHAPTER 4: PRE-INTERVIEW PREPARATION: RESUME AND COVER LETTER 15

CHAPTER 5: WHAT ARE YOU BRINGING TO THIS ORGANISATION? 31

CHAPTER 6: THINGS TO DO BEFORE YOUR INTERVIEW.... 37

CHAPTER 7: ENCOUNTER DIFFERENT INTERVIEWS 41

CHAPTER 8: WRITING A RESUME 49

CHAPTER 9: KNOW THE BASICS 59

CHAPTER 10: WHAT NOT TO DO 79

CHAPTER 11: GET TO THERE EARLY 89

CHAPTER 12: THREE MISTAKES PEOPLE MAKE DURING AN INTERVIEW 94

CHAPTER 13: FACE TO FACE INTERVIEWS 105

CHAPTER 14: EDUCATION QUESTIONS 116

CHAPTER 15: WHAT YOU WILL BRING TO THE POSITION 128

CHAPTER 16: HOW TO GROW IN YOUR CAREER WHILE WORKING TOWARDS YOUR DREAM JOB........................ 144

CHAPTER 17: WHAT TO DO WHEN YOU GET THERE?...... 150

CHAPTER 18: GETTING TO THE VENUE............................ 153

CHAPTER 19: PRESENTATION - SOLUTION 160

CHAPTER 20: TIPS FOR TELEPHONE INTERVIEWS............ 164

CHAPTER 21: ASK QUESTIONS 168

CHAPTER 22: QUESTIONS YOU SHOULD BE PREPARED TO ANSWER AT JOB INTERVIEW 173

CHAPTER 23: MAKE A GREAT FIRST IMPRESSION 184

CHAPTER 24: COVERING LETTER..................................... 190

CHAPTER 25: NUANCES OF EFFECTIVE COMMUNICATION SKILLS.. 196

CONCLUSION... 201

Introduction

Over his numerous movies, Rocky Balboa has always said that the real opponent has always been yourself. This line becomes especially relevant when it comes to job interviews.

Most people dread having to prepare for an interview because they aren't sure of what they'll be asked or how to conduct themselves during such an event. Because of these uncertainties, nervousness gets to them and it causes them to underperform and lose out on opportunities for employment.

This manual was designed for that specific problem. The only way to combat a serious case of the nerves is to prepare like there is no tomorrow. That is exactly what you're getting from this book.

Through this book, you will find information pertaining to almost every aspect of the job interview. You will learn what to expect, what to wear, how to act and most importantly, how to answer.

And it's not just how to answer, but to also make the most out of every opportunity to impress your would-be employer.

It is advised that you read this book from start to finish and highlight the particular sections that pose the highest interest to you. This book has been designed to take you from an unprepared applicant to a confident near hire.

Good luck!

Chapter 1: Basic Tips For A Great Job Interview

When preparing for an interview, it is best to begin by getting knowledge of some essential tips. Your maximum concentration on these tips is required no matter how experienced you are. These are the best tips for achieving a great result in your job interview:

1. Research the industry and the company

Ensure to do proper research of the company and the type of productive activities they engage in before going for an interview. As we can never predict where the interview questions would come from. It could be concerning productive events, its competitors, or even its position in the industry. The advantage would be your distinct ability to answer all these questions if you had done proper research concerning that company.

2. Get Some Sleep

Getting some more sleep is an essential factor in this situation as it helps you aim for quantity and quality. Interviews are always lengthy. Usually, an hour or over an hour as the case may be. So getting some more sleep will help sharpen your brain and enable it to give the correct answers to every interview question you are asked.

3. Check your Online Presence and Your Social Media Profiles

One thing that matters a lot to your interviewer is your online presence and social media profile, as it speaks a lot about the company if you are eventually employed. To ensure your social media is a safe place for everyone to visit. Correctly remove any sensitive pictures or write-ups like complaints about your relationship, sexually-provocative images, video clips from a party attended, etc. as these will reduce your chances of securing the job if found by your interviewer.

4. Always Wear a Confident Smile

A confident smile is considered an essential and necessary tip as far as the interview is concerned. When you know what you want, go for it with sure as a smile is inevitable as "Your smile is your Logo."

5. Silent Your Mobile Phone

Ensure to silent your mobile phone during an interview to avoid unexpected phone calls and notifications as these things speak of how professional you are to your interviewer, and you don't want to make the wrong impression, do you? However, the need to add a contact or place a reminder of an appointment may arise; therefore, do not switch off your phone.

6. Eat something before the interview

Always eat something light before an interview to avoid feeling weak or an embarrassing stomach growl from hunger during the interview. Eating dense food or drinking too much water to an interview is not advisable.

7. Arrive Early

Arriving earlier than the appointed time for an interview is very important as you might experience some unexpected encounters like traffic, inability to locate the right venue or the need to use the restroom. As we all know, no interviewer likes to be kept waiting.

8. Control your Body Language

During an interview, body postures like chewing your lips, stammering, fidgeting with an object should be avoided as this tells the interviewer how relaxed or anxious you are. Your body gestures, postures, and language matter a lot, so master proper positions like standing with your back straight.

Chapter 2: Suit Up!

Recently, it has been observed by employers that applicants tend to be a bit too "outlandish" in terms of what they wear during the interview. There are a lot of them who show up in their interview wearing they favorite jeans and sweat shirts. There are others who expose their piercings and wear heavy hair wax to maintain the "spikiness" of their hair. Employers even find it more disturbing to see applicants who are chewing gum wearing shirts that are not ironed and pants that are on the brink of falling down. What these applicants do not know is the fact that it is what they wear that resulted to their failure to get their dream jobs.

When showing up for an interview, you need to dress your best. It truly makes a big difference in most cases. Imagine two applicants who are equally qualified and equally skilled. If one of them is dressed to impress and the other is too casual, the employer is compelled to choose the one whose get up is impressive. It seems like he wants the job better than the other.

Most businesses employ a conservative atmosphere. While it may not be perfectly acceptable, appearance does matter in all kinds of businesses. Maybe in other environments, the climate may not be that conservative, so proper decorum might not be regarded as much. But if you are working in the context that you are still courting the employer's attention, it makes perfect sense that you dress well and suit up for your scheduled interview.

Experts say, "when in doubt, dwell on the conservative side." Being conservative is the safest assumption. "Better overdressed rather than underdressed," they all say. If you are a bit overdressed, at least, it is a product of too much preparation. On the other hand, if you are underdressed, it is a manifestation that you failed to prepare. If you are an employer, you would probably know who to favor in such a situation.

The perception on a person is determined by his looks. Fifty five percent of one's valuation of his self-worth and dignity is attributed to his looks. Therefore, one should dress up properly, especially for a job interview.

If you are a lady, the following are the best things to wear:

A conservative suit which has a solid color

A blouse that is color coordinated

Closed shoes

A bit of jewelry (not too much, please)

A very neat hairdo that communicates professionalism

Very little trace of perfume and sparse amount of makeup

Nails that are clean and manicured

A briefcase containing your portfolio

On the other hand, the following is the preferred attire for men:

- A conservative solid colored suit
- Long sleeve shirt, preferably white in color
- A tie that matches your suit and shirt
- Black socks matched with leather shoes
- No jewelry, except the necessary ones (wedding/engagement ring, etc.)
- Professional-looking and very clean hairstyle
- Not too much aftershave because the smell can be distracting
- Trimmed nails
- A briefcase containing your professional portfolio

Chapter 3: Things To Do Before A Job Interview

Before D-Day

The night before the interview, make sure that you have the following information. You can request this when you are invited to an interview by phone or email a week or a couple days earlier.

1) Test venue. Although the company will automatically provide this information without being asked, it is completely all right to ask for details about the test location, including the street name, building name, room number, transportation route, etc. If possible, visit the venue a couple of days earlier to estimate the time needed to get there.

2) Test schedule. Don't forget to ask them when the test will be conducted. This includes exact date and time.

3) Test format. You could also ask whether they will hold all the recruitment tests (skills and psychological tests and interview) on the same day or on separate days.

4) Items to bring. Ask them whether you should bring specific items such as HB or 2B pencils, etc. Make sure that you have put all the necessary items, including pens (at least two just in case), notebook, CV or resume, ID, etc., in your bag or purse.

5) Prepare your clothes the night before an interview. Just to be safe, wear a formal shirt so you will look neat and professional. Remember first impressions are very important.

6) Get familiar with the position. Read the job description carefully, including the scope of work, requirements, and so on.

7) Do a little research on the company you are applying to. This is important and extremely useful during an interview. The interviewers will be glad if you know a little bit about their company. This proves

that you are a creative person and full of initiative.

D-Day Checklist

1) Make sure that you have your breakfast before going to an interview. This is important because you have to be physically and emotionally fit throughout the tests. Sometimes, a company holds all the tests, including the skills and psychological tests and interview, on a single day. This may take from early morning until late afternoon, and not infrequently, there will be a long wait between each test.

This is done intentionally to test your physical and emotional strengths. They want to ensure that you can handle pressure and stress and manage to stay focus and think logically even when you're feeling depressed, hungry, tired, and angry.

Don't expect a recruitment test to be as quick and simple as school examinations, where you arrive, wait a couple minutes, complete the test and then go home.

You have to demonstrate to them that you're strong, both physically and emotionally. With proper preparation, you will eventually get a job.

2) Get up early and NEVER ever arrive late for an interview. Arrive around 15-30 minutes early so you can catch your breath and relax. Keep practicing the interview questions and answers on your way to the test location.

3) DON'T smoke or chew gum.

Chapter 4: Pre-Interview Preparation: Resume And Cover Letter

Obviously, before you can secure a job interview, you must prepare a winning resume and, typically speaking, write an engaging cover letter. These two elements are the most significant documents you will ever create in your quest for the ideal job. The two sections below will take you through both processes with some basic guidelines and handy tips for how to stand out from other applicants, securing that all-important interview.

Building the Best Resume

Building your resume is, really, a two-part process: first, you have to acquire education, experience, and skills that are appropriate to put into a resume; second, you have to understand how to assemble that information in an impressive, professional, and attractive manner. In the first case, think about your experiences and skills in the broadest manner possible: clearly, educational accomplishments are important, but other activities and experiences can also apply to a variety of job requirements. Especially if you don't have a wide variety of experience yet, think of how even minor things that you have done could be applicable to certain skills attractive to a job market (leadership, independent thinking, and teamwork). In the second case, there are numerous tips and techniques that you can follow in order to build the most impressive, most readable, and most successful resume.

First, if the sincerest form of flattery is an imitation, then flatter some successful job seekers out there and review some examples. You need not build your resume completely from scratch; the internet provides a plethora of samples for you to review and to adjust according to your own needs. Be sure to review samples that are relevant to your field, as different fields have different standards. Second, if you are feeling apprehensive about creating your own resume, especially if this is your first attempt, then use a template. Again, the internet is awash with templates (most of them are free) that can help get you started. Do be aware, however, that the template is just the base on which you build: customize it to fit your specific experience and personal story.

Third, consider the format of the resume, as well as the field. Resumes can be organized chronologically (this is perhaps most common), listing educational and professional achievements and positions in the order at which they occurred, from most recent on down. However, there are other types of resumes: a functional resume, for instance, lists skills and abilities with relevant examples, rather than a chronological work history; a targeted resume is one that is "targeted" specifically to one particular position so that it lists only skills and work experience relevant to the specific job itself. A combination resume would do some sort of mixture of the aforementioned.

Always include contact information, though this no longer means that you need to provide a physical address (with so many workplaces themselves not adhering to one particular physical address and the growth of remote work, this has become moot). It's fine to use Gmail, as long as the address is professional; create a new account if you have to. You should also include links to other professional sites at which you are associated, such as LinkedIn or other social media that you utilize for professional purposes.

Relevant to the above point, you can create your own website for professional purposes: if your resume feels agonizingly short—and most employers prefer shorter resumes—then creating a personal, professional site is one way in which you can tell more of your story before landing the interview itself. Provide a link to this space on your resume, and allow your prospective employer to peruse it at will. This has become ever more important in the "gig" economy.

Back to the resume itself, be sure to make it as "skimmable" as possible: while we all want to believe that each prospective employer reads our hard-won accomplishments with great care and thoroughness, they probably do not, especially for highly competitive fields. Some ways in which you can make your information easily readable are as follows:

use a basic font, such as Times New Roman or Arial;

don't justify your margins, which creates odd gaps in formatting;

keep dates and other numbers aligned to the right;

use digits when employing numbers (10, rather than ten);

avoid entering any information;

use boldface to highlight either the company for whom you worked or your respective roles at previous workplaces, but not both;

avoid all caps;

when using bullet points, keep it to two lines or less;

employ a separate section for skills, so prospective employers can read through quickly;

and be consistent in formatting throughout your resume, leaving some white space for ease of reading.

Always start with the most recent relevant work experience and work your way backward chronologically. Typically speaking, you should only include the last decade of work experience (up to fifteen years is acceptable) and only work experience that is relevant to the position to which you are currently applying. That said, be sure to use space wisely: you may have done a college internship that is more relevant to the current position under consideration than your previous work experience. Customize thoughtfully.

If you don't necessarily have a lot—or any!—work experience in the field to which you are applying, you need not give up. This is the occasion to create a functional resume, wherein you list relevant skills and activities you have acquired and experienced that fit with the job. This is also the occasion to write a strong cover letter that will detail why you are, in fact, a good fit for a job in which you have little professional experience (see the following chapter for advice on creating strong cover letters).

While the most effective resumes will showcase your "soft skills"—such as good communication and strong leadership—they will do so in a direct and active manner. That is, don't simply state that you have effective communication skills, formulate a bullet point under a relevant work experience that demonstrates how you employed effective communication skills or strong leadership on the job. Specificity is key, and it allows you to stand out far more than fancy fonts or colorful graphics.

Also remember that work experience doesn't always have to indicate traditional, paid employment: if you have volunteered for years at a facility or for an organization that has relevance to the job position, then, by all means, consider including this experience in your work history. This is part of what will make you an effective employee and a passionate contributor—in fact, this kind of work often showcases your passion to a greater degree. Next, move onto the education section of your resume and keep it in reverse chronological order, with the most recent first. Also, you should always list your work experience first, unless you have just graduated from college or other educational institution. Work experience will almost always be more relevant to your current job search than your college education.

While numbers can be important to work

experience—showing how long you were employed at a particular job, or revealing a particular salary range—it is less important in an educational experience. When you graduated is not as relevant as the fact that you did graduate, and your GPA is less important than your achievements and honors along the way. You might also consider listing special skills or achievements in a separate section, space permitting. This is your opportunity to show that you have excelled in particular areas (such as learning a second language or getting an award for achievement in your field) or that you have acquired specialized skills (such as knowing HTML or Java). Finally, be sure to address any red flags or gaps in your resume: these are fine to discuss within the interview itself, of course, but you should be aware of them and prepared to discuss them in honest detail.

Creating a Compelling Cover Letter

Along with the resume, the cover letter is the most significant part of the pre-interview process: a cover letter showcases who you are and why you would be the best fit for this particular job. Not every job application requires a cover letter, but most professional level positions do—even if they don't require it, it's often a good idea to prepare one, just in case, as it can often help you organize your thoughts when preparing for an interview. Many people dread writing a cover letter—there are overwhelming numbers of examples online—but it can be both beneficial to you and to your potential employer. In fact, some employers rely on the cover letter more than the resume to decide who to select for the interview process; it is an equally important part of your desire to land that ideal job.

One of the most fundamental bits of advice that anyone could receive regarding writing cover letters is to craft an individual and specific cover letter for each job application. While this might sound like a lot of work—and it potentially is—it is the only way to ensure that you are perceived as someone who is knowledgeable and passionate about this particular position. Address the cover letter to your interviewer, hiring manager, or potential employer, when possible, and customize the letter to address the requirements requested and the skills you possess that will allow you to thrive in the job. Some research into the company (this is addressed in the following chapter) may also help you in crafting the perfect cover letter for a particular company. Having said the above, it is still appropriate to use a template to get started or to recycle a handful of words or phrases for each cover letter. The trick is to avoid sounding generic: like using "To Whom It May Concern" or "I am applying for a position (rather than noting which) at your company"—these are vague and reveal a lack of interest on your part. If you don't know the name of the person to whom you should address the letter, then resort to something else more specific than "To Whom It May Concern." For example, you could address the letter to "Department Hiring Manager" or "Executive Search Committee," again specifying which department or position that your search would fall under. One of the first mistakes you must avoid when writing a cover letter is a rehashing ground that is already in your resume. The cover letter is the place where you can expand upon the basics of employment position and time period and allow your accomplishments and personality shine. When thinking about how to construct a cover letter that reveals a fuller portrait of you as an employee, ask yourself some pointed questions: choose a particular activity mentioned on your resume, and ask yourself how you approached implementing this task, what skills it called upon; ask yourself what specific details are important to understanding how you accomplished a particular task or landed a specific job; finally, ask yourself what parts of your personality were key in how you landed and handled a specific job and/or task. These kinds of questions not only help you craft a stronger cover letter, but they also prepare you for the interview that will surely come.

Be sure to focus on the skills and experiences you have that are directly relevant to the position—and to the larger company. Avoid suggesting how wonderful the job would be for **you**—certainly, any hiring manager will be aware of what is at stake for a potential hire—but do mention what you would bring to the company, the department, and/or the group.

The cover letter is also the place wherein you can make the case that you are the ideal fit for a particular position—even if you don't necessarily have the employment history to back it up. That is, you can really showcase your skillset here, to show your potential employer exactly what it is that you have to offer, even if your resume is either thin or disparate from the exact position you're aiming to get.

In terms of tone, there is a balancing act to strike: on the one hand, you are writing a professional piece for a professional purpose; on the other hand, you are trying to come across as a personable and pleasant person who will fit in with a larger team or company. Excessive formality makes you seem stiff and distant, while too much conversational personality can appear sloppy or flippant. You want to appear approachable and professional.

This is also a moment at which the research you've done on the company (see the following chapter for more on that) comes in handy: craft your cover letter using the style and lingo of the company to which you're applying. Read their web site and absorb some of their keywords and phrases—beware of overdoing this, as it can sound sycophantic, but it does show that you would be a good fit.

Edit carefully, proofread thoroughly: a cover letter with errors is a blatant dead end. Have someone else read it if you fear your writing skills are not quite up to par. Last, this is one of the single most significant pieces of advice that you can get for any piece of writing you are doing: READ IT ALOUD before your final edit and submission. Reading aloud can help you capture the tone (is it too stiff and formal? Too conversational?) and flow (is it too rambling? well organized?), as well as alert you to mistakes (if you're gasping for breath at the end of a sentence, then it probably needs some editing). By the time you are called in for the interview, you should know your cover letter like your own reflection—because, indeed, that's what it is, a reflection of who you are, and will be as an ideal employee.

Finally, be sure to keep a master list of all the jobs for which you have applied, as well as copies of the particular resumes and cover letters that you ultimately send out. Always keep your basic template in place, but save versions of the basic resume and cover letter that are customized to each particular job search.

Chapter 5: What Are You Bringing To This Organisation?

From The Perspective Of The Candidate

The easiest way to prepare for this sort of question is to research and find out where the organisation is trying to go, where they are heading, their plans for the future and what they say they need to do to get there. Which new activities, business operations, new products, new systems are coming on board? Then ask yourself, which skills or knowledge do you have, needed by the organisation, to reach those goals? All employers are happy to have employees whose skills or knowledge will help the organisation move into the future. Understand that it's not all about skill — It's also about relevant, usable, progressive knowledge.

If you are just graduating from university or hold a professional qualification, you may not have a skill but more crucially, a certain new knowledge that will be a useful ingredient in the potential employer's future operations – this is your ace card, use it. So remember: Try matching the future direction of the organisation with the skills or knowledge you have which may be good ingredients for that direction – that is what you are bringing to the organisation; an ingredient for their present or future success. It's a subtle way of saying that you understand that the organisation needs to move forward, you have a fair idea where it is moving and what is needed to get there and that you have "SOME" of the needed inputs to get it there – that's progressive recruitment.

From The Perspective Of The Employer

This is the one question that will make a lot of candidates feel deflated or defeated. Interestingly however, it is the one question which enables interviewers to see the candidate's confidence and his/her ability to demonstrate a clear understanding of who s/he believes the potential employer is looking for in the role. When the interviewer starts hearing generic answers like **"I am hardworking" or "I am a team player"** etc., they will soon recognise the candidate either doesn't know what it is the organisation is looking for, or hasn't carefully assessed what s/he is capable of offering the role, should they get it. It is a question which will also test the candidate's ability to demonstrate that their past experiences are usable in the organisation's current state, or if s/he is dynamic and understands trends in business. They may further highlight their skills, experiences etc. which may not be useful now but soon will be in the future.

Finally, it tells the interviewer point-blank if the candidate can "sell" convincingly. Being able to sell is entirely different from being a sales person. If you can sell yourself, you can sell anything. It also shows persuasion skills. And don't be fooled – employers know that business is really all about selling – everybody is selling, from the shop floor person trying to convince customers to buy the company's products or services to the chief executive trying to convince the entire organisation that his new direction will work, given the support.

HOW DID YOU FIND OUT ABOUT THIS JOB?

From The Perspective Of The Candidate

This is one of those questions you really can't lie about, but my suggestion is that if it is possible, decide where you want your career to go. Is it auditing, accountancy, consultancy, banking, human resource, development, training etc? Once you have determined that, start looking for jobs in the right places. Employers who want the best HR personnel are more likely to advertise excellent positions in magazines, websites or similar platforms which are subscribed to by HR enthusiasts. The same applies to other career paths. For some employers, potential employees who read their adverts on these types of platforms appear to them as being more focused and more discerning. They appear to potential employers as people who know where to look for the right things. However, where these kinds of targeted newsletters, magazines, internet sites or platforms don't exist in your particular country, don't worry, this question won't be taking too many marks away from you. The other angle to it is this – if you heard about the role from a friend, colleague, family, etc – there is a high chance that you are the kind of person with good human relations and therefore you are good at keeping and managing your contacts – this is a superior skill for any employee to have.

From The Perspective Of The Employer

This question is quite deceptive. To the candidate, it is a straightforward question and nothing to lie about (no sense in doing so), but to the interviewer it provides tremendous insight, depending also on where an advert was placed. A candidate who learnt about the job by word of mouth in social circles or through colleagues is likely to be considered by the employer as having strong relationship building skills. Learning about the job from a niche publication such as an industry specific magazine rather than a widely public newspaper may indicate that s/he is very discerning or focused. On the other hand any indication that the job was referred to the candidate by someone in the organisation is likely to mean that they have already been investigating the organisation or at least have been talking to someone about it.

Chapter 6: Things To Do Before Your Interview

Plan what you will wear to your interview, set it out the night before. This will alleviate the stress level on the day of your interview.

Dress neatly and conservatively. No cut off shorts, jeans with holes in them. I know that's in style. Save it for personal time. It is not work appropriate. Have clean, ironed clothes. Wrinkles look like you slept in them then raced to the interview.

If you can't take the time to be presentable for the interview, you're would be boss knows you won't be presentable on the job, as a reflection of his company or business.

Research the business. Knowing facts about the company helps when you are making small talk with the person interviewing you. The fact that you took the time to learn about something so important to your boss, means you will take pride in the company or business when hired as an employee.

Have copies of your resume' and references ready to go the night before the interview. Don't wait until the day of to make copies. This is always when the printer runs out of ink or paper. Technical difficulties love to catch us at the worst moment. It must be an unwritten rule in tech land or something.

Prepare early, not at the last minute to keep your stress level down so you're not late. Be early. Don't just try to be on time. Plan to be early. This takes in to account last minute issues. Traffic, needing gas, any number of little things.

Plan a few questions to ask them. Usually you will be asked, "do you have any questions?" If you say no, it may come across like you are indifferent.

A few great questions to ask, if you can't come up with any would be...

Ask: What are some opportunities for advancement in thisdepartment?

Ask: Why did the person before me leave the job?

Ask: How long will my training time be if I am hired?

Ask: Can you describe a typical workday for this position?

Ask: When will you be making a final decision?

Ask: Does this company have a welcoming environment?

Never ask about salary. If it wasn't clear when you applied, wait until you are offered the job. Do not bring it up at the interview, especially a group interview. The salary or hourly rate may not be the same for every applicant. Even if there are several openings of the same type of job being filled. There are different levels of experienced job seekers, this will determine what the pay is, unless it is a set rate regardless of experience. In this case it's usually stated in the job posting. That will weed out applicants that would not be interested based on rate of pay. No need to waste your time or theirs.

Time is money I am sure you have heard that. It's because it's true. Someone gets paid to go through all those job applications and perform these background checks then schedule job interviews & drug tests. There is quite a bit of Human Resources work behind the scenes happening.

Finally moving on to chapter four ~ Top interview questions.

Chapter 7: Encounter Different Interviews

Interviewers use several different types of interviews, questions, and techniques to determine your capabilities. Therefore, it is to your advantage to be well prepared for a variety of possible interview situations, questions, and techniques as well as different types of interviews. It is always better to be prepared for both expected and unexpected interviews and interviewers than to blow the interview because you were caught off guard with a surprise interview. You may, for example, interview several times with a single employer or have a single interview with several individuals.

Some interviewers are seasoned professionals who know how to conduct good interviews. Others may be amateurs who know little about how to elicit or convey the information both you and the organization need to make the best decision. Before examining how to prepare for a successful interview, let's look at various types of employment interviews. You should be aware of these since you may unexpectedly encounter one of the less frequent interview types sometime during the interview process.

If you are asked to return for a second or third interview with the same organization, you may face a different type of interview than during the first round of interviews. This brings up an important point. Thus far, we have referred to a successful job interview. For many positions especially professional or management-level positions you will face more than one interview. In some cases, you will go through three or four interviews. Each interview may consist of interviews with several individuals.

3.1 Interview Types

You may encounter several types of interviews throughout the course of your job search. Central to our interview typology is a concern with the objectives or goals of interviewers. While your ultimate goal is to get the right job, you may also have other goals. From the interviewee's perspective, other objectives may include gathering information about the job opening; acquiring advice about your job search if the present opening doesn't seem to be a good fit with your skills, abilities, and knowledge; receiving referrals for job openings that may be more appropriate within this firm or with other firms; or getting invitations to additional interviews. In the end, pursuing these goals may be more important to your job search than getting a job offer for the opening you came hoping to fill.

3.1.1 Informational/Networking

Some interviews are often overlooked by job seekers. Informational/networking interviews are an important step toward the ultimate goal of landing the job. Once you have an objective and identify what you do well and enjoy doing, you should talk with people working in your area of interest. Such interviews will give you valuable information about particular jobs and careers, especially the skills and experience employers expect you to have for different jobs. This type of interview also yields important job information and helps develop referral networks. The networks consist of individuals who serve as job contacts in your field of interest. Best of all, these interviews often lead directly to formal job interviews.

3.1.2 Screening Interviews

Employment interviews are normally conducted when there are actual or anticipated job openings. The first such interview is often a screening interview. The employer's goal is as the term implies - screen people in or out of further consideration. For example, an employer may have a pool of ten promising applicants. Wishing to narrow the number for face-to-face interviews, the employer calls each candidate to inquire about their employment status, gather more information on their qualifications, and identify cues regarding their appropriateness for the position. These telephone interviews will result in eliminating most of the applicants.

3.1.3 Videoconferencing

Video conferencing interviews are used for many of the same reasons as the telephone screening interview. They save time and money. They allow the employer to get impressions of the candidate without the expense of flying a candidate in for an interview. Since video conferencing allows the interviewer to see as well as hear the candidate, it provides more information than a telephone interview.

3.1.4 Electronic Screening Interviews

A new method for screening job applicants is the use of computerized questions to elicit information before the applicant meets the hiring official. For this interview, the applicant is requested to sit at a computer terminal and respond to a series of questions that will also be "scored" electronically. Though used at present primarily by larger firms, the method may "catch on." If you face this situation, you should do better if you have some understanding of what is taking place. This electronic screening method has several advantages. First, the computer presentation poses the same questions in the same way to all applicants and will "score" the responses, thus supposedly taking some of the subjectivity out of this portion of the interview.

3.1.5 Selection/Hiring Interviews

Many people think of the selection/hiring interview as the "real interview." In many respects, it is. This interview will be conducted in greater depth than the screening interview. It also will have greater consequences for you and your future. Most applicants expect only one person to conduct the selection/hiring interview and expect it to take place in an office setting. Although perhaps this is the most common format, these interviews can vary in terms of the number of people involved as well as different settings.

There are five basic formats for hiring interviews. They are a one-to-one, sequential, serial, panel, or a group interview.

3.1.6 One-to-One

One-to-one, or face-to-face interviews are the most common type encountered by interviewees. The applicant and the employer meet, usually at the employer's office, and sit down to discuss the position and the applicant's skills, knowledge, and abilities as they relate to the job. At some point, though hopefully late in the interview, salary considerations, as well as other benefits, may be discussed.

3.1.7 Sequential Interviews

For many positions, especially those beyond entry-level, more than one interview will be necessary. Sequential interviews are simply a series of interviews with the decision being made to screen the candidate in or out after each interview. The candidates who are screened in are called back for additional interviews. Although each of the sequential interviews is most frequently a one-to-one interview, you could meet with more than one interviewer at the same time in any of these sessions. You may meet with the same person in each interview, but it is more likely you will meet new people in subsequent interviews.

Chapter 8: Writing A Resume

As you begin to write your resume, you'll need to make some choices about your structure. First, you need to decide which type of resume to write. Next, you need to choose which of the traditional parts of a resume you will include. After you've chosen a format and parts and written the resume, you'll also need to make sure your work adheres to a time-tested set of dos and don'ts that are designed to present you in the most professional manner possible. Each of these steps is outlined in the following sections. Keep the previous chapter's advice in mind, and if you get stuck at any point, remember you can always ask your peers for feedback. They may not be experts in resume writing, but they are likely to catch mistakes, omissions, or problems you have not noticed.

Types of Resumes

Chronological Resume

The chronological resume is perhaps most common, and it is generally accepted as the resume format preferred by employers. In a chronological resume, positions held are listed reverse chronologically (with the present or most recently held position listed first), and a brief description of job duties, skills, and responsibilities is included with each position. The benefit of this type of resume is that it allows the employer to quickly note which jobs an applicant has held and when. For recent college graduates, those with large work gaps, and career changers, this type of resume may not be the right choice as it has a tendency to highlight a lack of experience. For those with a strong work history in their field, however, the chronological resume is an excellent choice.

Functional Resume

A functional resume de-emphasizes positions held, instead spotlighting the skills a job seeker has acquired. Skills are organized by type (e.g., "technical skills") and exact job titles, and dates are omitted. Using this format, a job seeker can showcase all the skillsets he or she has, whether gained from work, schooling or volunteer experience, without drawing attention to gaps in work history or the fact that he or she has no direct experience in the field. Note, though that many employers do not accept this type of resume; they cannot, for example, see where the applicant has worked, which is an enormous drawback.

Combination Resume

Career changers and others who'd like to avoid the chronological resume might consider the combination resume, which is created by placing skill groupings first, as with a functional resume, then including a reverse chronological job history directly after the skills section. By including both, you are showing employers that you have a useful bank of skills and that you have a work history. If you choose this format, beware of making the skills section so long that the experience section is pushed to the second page — employers may bother to flip over to find your job history.

Parts of a Resume

Contact Information

No matter which type of resume you choose, your contact information should be placed at the top. At minimum, the information should include your name, address (including state and zip code), telephone number, and email address. Depending on the industry, you may also wish to include a fax number or Skype name.

Objective or Summary

A solid objective or summary can excite a reader's interest and should give just enough clear, concise information to encourage the reader to want to know more. An objective states the type of position the candidate is seeking: "To gain an entry-level position in sales with a company that values customer retention and substantial production of cold business." A summary gives a short overview of achievements, strong points, and experience: "Motivated sales professional with 20 years of experience and an average client retention rate of 85 percent. Comfortable working without supervision but also a team player. Interested in building sales skills through professional development." Most resumes include one or the other; those with impressive professional experience might opt for the latter. Job seekers who choose to include an objective should be careful not to make it too vague or restricting.

Work Experience

This section is where employers look to determine whether you've been employable in the past. For each position, you should include the name of the company, the location (city and state), the years you held the position (or months if it was less than a year), and your job title. Under each position, you may list the duties you had, using past tense unless you still hold the position. As with every other part of the resume, you are not required to write in full sentences; in fact, brevity is preferred.

Education

Information in the education section should start with the highest degree you attained and include the name of the institution, the location (city and state), the title of the degree, and the year the degree was earned. If you have not graduated yet, you should include the expected date of graduation, and if you did not graduate, you can simply list the types of courses you participated in. If your GPA was impressive, above at least a 3.5, then you may include it, but it is not necessary. Recent college graduates who don't have any work experience are generally expected to place the education section above the work history or skills section.

Awards or Achievements

You may be proud that you earned a yellow belt in karate, but this information probably isn't pertinent to a potential employer. Only include this section, if you have won awards, gained skills, or participated in events that your employer will care about or need; such as the ability to speak multiple languages.

References

The standard line to include under references is "References available upon request." Since most employers assume they can ask you for references, however, you are not obligated to include this section. In the interest of preparation, you should consider creating a separate document that lists your references that you can give to a potential employer along with your resume at his or her request.

Dos and Don'ts Of Resume Writing

Dos

-Do ask yourself questions a hiring manager is likely to ask, and write with the goal of answering these questions.

-Do edit your resume meticulously, checking for grammar, spelling, and punctuation errors. If correcting your written work is not your strong point, ask a friend or colleague for help.

-Do tweak your resume before sending it to different employers to highlight the skills and experience they are each looking for.

-Do use action words — "contributed to a team" not "was on a team."

Don'ts

-Don't use an offensive or childish email address for your resume.

-Don't lie about your skills and promise more than you can deliver.

-Don't include a photo unless you work in an industry where the way a person looks has some bearing on the job (such as acting).

-Don't include overly personal information, such as your political leanings.

-Don't use sweeping generalities. Give concrete information — "added $500,000 in revenue streams in 2012" instead of "increased business."

Job seekers who are armed with a strong, polished resume are one step ahead of their peers. You are not finished writing yet, though. Your resume is not the only document most companies will want to see; you are also going to need to write cover letters.

Chapter 9: Know The Basics

A. Three Primary Inquiries

Know the nuts and bolts. There are just three primary inquiries a questioner needs to inquire:

Will you carry out the employment?

Will you carry out the occupation?

Will you fit in?

Organizing your arranging around these three ranges, will help you to cover the most critical issues prone to be secured amid the meeting, and give you the opportunity to set up your key articulations and reactions to market yourself most successfully.

Inquiries around there are planned to test your experience. It is improbable you would have been welcomed for meeting if your capabilities and experience on paper did not coordinate the criteria for the employment. Most questioners thusly will spend around 15% of the meeting on this region.

Do you have the obliged capabilities?

In the event that the employment is extremely specialized, you may be obliged to exhibit more prominent top to bottom specialized information in the meeting. Be arranged to check and go down any cases you make with respect to capabilities et cetera. Superintendents are progressively utilizing the administrations of information offices to confirm points of interest given on CVs and application shapes. Keep away from 'harmless untruths, for example, updating your A Level results. A little lie discovered will undermine your believability completely.

B. Typical Interview Questions and Answers

Here is common/typical interview and tips how to answer them best.

1. Why would you like to work for this organization? Why are you keen on this occupation?

The interviewer is trying to determine what you know and like about the company, whether you will be willing to make a commitment to the job, and if your skills match the job requirements. Your exploration will be a major help in forming your response to this inquiry. Say as many positive things about the company as possible, demonstrate your enthusiasm for whatever items/administrations they offer and clarify why the position fits with your vocation objectives.

2. Have you done this sort of work some time recently?

The interviewer needs to know whether you can figure out how to carry out the employment in a sensible time and the amount of preparing you will require. Never say "no" to this inquiry. Rather, stretch the experience you do have that will help you in taking in the new occupation rapidly and productively. No two employments are indistinguishable and you never do precisely the same work. In all occupations, new abilities, standards and points of interest must be found out. Make certain to specify the accompanying:

Your past work experience.

Your training and preparing identified with the occupation.

Volunteer work that might relate to the job.

Any transferable skills - e.g. organizational skills, people skills.

Your ability to learn quickly and how quickly you learned that type of work in the past.

3. What kind of training or qualifications do you have?

The interviewer is trying to find out what school credentials you have. If you have no formal school qualifications but have a lot of experience, you might say:

I didn't get formal school training for this employment however I have (number) of years of involvement in the field. I'm willing to learn new abilities or go to class to get further preparing in the event that I am offered the occupation. I learn rapidly and I like to continue overhauling my aptitudes. If you have just completed a training course but have little work experience, you might say:

I took a one year preparing program in (name of system) at (name of school) which is identified with the occupation I'm requesting. I look forward to working in the field and putting into practice what I learned. I don't have a lot of work experience in this area but I learn quickly. I know you will be happy with my work.

4. Tell me about yourself. Why should we hire you?

The questioner is attempting to get some answers concerning you, your employment aptitudes and how well you convey what needs be. Try not to harp on individual issues. State you're most ideally equipped capabilities for the occupation. Be particular and incorporate samples to backing your announcements. Attempt to demonstrate that you meet the superintendent's desires. For instance:

I am reliable, trustworthy and can be tallied upon to complete what I begin. I get a lot of fulfilment from realizing that I have done something great and on time. For instance, at my present occupation, I was given distinctive work arranges consistently. It was my obligation to complete the requests and verify they all met quality and security models inside of a particular due date. Once in a while, I needed to acclimate myself with the item and the creation process. I was constantly ready to learn rapidly and complete my employment obligations.

5. What do you do in your extra time?

Interviewers ask this question to see if your activities and hobbies might help the company and to get an idea of what kind of person you are outside your work life. Describe any volunteer work you do and any hobbies or interests that might relate to the job in some way. Stick to dynamic interests, for example, playing games, carpentry, gardening, and so forth. Abstain from saying idle and non-inventive exercises, for example, sitting in front of the TV.

6. What do you think of working in a group?

The interviewer is trying to find out about your ability to get along with others. Focus on the following:

The advantage of working in a group is that the various individuals in a group complement one another in carrying out certain tasks.

Give specific examples of your personal experience in a group

7. How do you react to instruction and criticism?

The questioner is attempting to discover how you coexist with Supervisors and how you feel about power. You may say:

"I acknowledge getting guideline and feedback when it is done reasonably and usefully."

8. With the kind of work experience you have had, do you think this job would bore you?

The questioner may think you are overqualified and need this job just until something better come along. Stress that no occupation is regularly exhausting in light of the fact that you generally learn new aptitudes. Say how you would advantage by functioning for the organization and the other way around.

9. Why did you choose this line of work?

The questioner is attempting to get some answers concerning your dedication to your vocation decision. At the end of the day do you do it on the grounds that you adore the work or simply accept any occupation you can get for the cash? If you did this work for many years and stopped due to a layoff, you might say:

"I have done this for (number) of years. I like my work. The main reason I cleared out my last work environment was on account of I was laid off."

10. How well do you work under pressure or tight deadlines?

This inquiry demonstrates that the occupation you're seeking will include working under weight. Give cases of volunteer and paid work that included weight and due dates. You could specify that we are constantly confronted with weight and due dates in our lives and you wouldn't fret the anxiety. Unpleasant circumstances are learning and testing background. You may specify the accompanying:

How you took care of vast surge orders at your last working environment.

How you arranged for exams and homework assignments while working full-time and going to class low maintenance.

How you dealt with an emergency circumstance. (For instance: a car accident)

11. How often were you absent from work in your last job? Have you ever had any serious illness or injuries? Do you have any health problems?

The interviewer is trying to find out if you have any health issues which will cause you to take a lot of sick days. You do not have to go into your health history for the interviewer. If you have health problems that do not interfere with your work performance, do not give the interviewer details about them. If you had a previous health problem that interfered with your work in the past, but is no longer a problem, do not volunteer this information. It no longer affects your work; therefore the employer does not have to know.

On the off chance that you have a wellbeing issue that will influence your work execution, clarify your circumstance quickly and stress the positive focuses. I will be useful to have a positive reference letter from your past manager. This letter ought to clarify the kind of obligations you did and stress that you are an enduring specialist who is mindful, persevering and dependable.

12. Are you bondable?

This question indicates that the job involves working with money or valuable merchandise. Likely the manager's insurance agency obliges that just bondable individuals be enlisted as a state of their protection policy. As long as you don't have a criminal record, and you have not beforehand been denied a bond, you ought to reply "yes" to this inquiry. Alert: If you answer yes when you are not lawfully bondable it is likely that the business will find this.

13. Have you ever been fired or quit a job?

The interviewer is looking for clues to any problems you have had in previous jobs and if you may have the same problems in a new job. Try to:

Abstain from saying anything negative in regards to yourself or your past business. In the event that you had issues, clarify them without being negative.

Be watchful not the utilization "terminated" or "quit". Rather utilize words, for example, "I changed jobs", "I was laid off", or "I needed a more challenging job".

If you were fired and are not on good terms with your previous employer, explain the reason why you were fired. Stress that you learned something from the previous situation.

14. Why haven't you worked recently?

The questioner is searching for signs to major issues or employment challenges that could continue to another occupation. You may say:

Since I was laid off from my past executive, I have been effectively searching for work. Be that as it may, as you probably are aware, there are numerous individuals searching for work and seeking the same employments. I have constantly worked consistently yet I haven't possessed the capacity to discover a vocation in the present employment market.

After I got laid off from my past boss, I chose to backtrack to class to overhaul my aptitudes so I can show signs of improvement, more secure employment.

15. What are your long-term goals or career plans?

The questioner may need to know whether you are aggressive, arrangement ahead, or on the off chance that you set objectives for yourself. The questioner might likewise need to recognize what desire you have of the organization. You may say:

I would like to end up great at my employment and maybe take some educating to wind up more talented in my field of work. I plan to learn (name of region or abilities) extremely well with the goal that I can be elevated to a higher position in (name aptitude or office).

16. What do you feel are your greatest strengths?

This is your opportunity to brag a little bit. It is important that you have done your research about the type of work that you are applying for. For example if you are applying as a production labourer and from your research you understand that this type of work required people that have the ability to meet quotas, work as a team and make improvement suggestions, then it is important for you to incorporate this into your strengths.

Illustration:

"My most noteworthy quality is that I have a ton of activity. I am continually searching for a superior approach to do things at work that I feel would spare the organization cash and I can simply accomplish my creation amounts. For instance one time I was working at my station and I felt that I was squandering time by continually needing to stroll to the opposite side of my station to get a few sections. So I revamped the station and my boss was truly inspired as it expanded my share."

17. What do you feel are your weaknesses?

You never need to give any sign of any weaknesses that you have. Turn you weaknesses into qualities by living up to expectations it to the executive's preference.

Examples:

"I am the kind of individual or is difficult for myself. I am continually anticipating that I should do a smidgen more. Then again, I figure this works out well for my boss. "

Or

"I never like to leave work until I have everything completed totally. Here and there this annoys me however I feel inside that it is critical. "

Or

"I am the sort of individual who dependably brings my work home with me. This occasionally meddles with my own life however I feel that work starts things out."

18. How would you describe your last employer?

Never rundown or say anything negative in regards to anyone or anybody. The manager will feel that you will do it to them. You ought to express the positive things, for example, he had elevated requirements and I truly regarded him for that. He was practical and truly knew the occupation I was doing, in the event that I had any issues he was receptive and would dependably give me recommendation or he gave the obligation to benefit a vocation.

Examples:

"I liked my employer. He/she treated me fairly and respected my work."

Or

"I admired my past business having given me the chance to procure a ton of abilities and encounters in (name territory of work ability)."

19. What five words would be describing you?

These ought to be your transferrable aptitudes, for example, dependable, timely, organized, friendly, legitimate, agreeable, active, and simple to coexist with, hardworking, energetic, take pride in my work, mindful, respected, and dedicated.

20. What did you like about your last job?

Say just positive things that you feel could exchange crosswise over to the position you are requisitioning.

Example:

"I enjoyed my last occupation in light of the fact that I coexisted well with my collaborators and the work was testing, quick paced and I was given a great deal of obligation to benefit a vocation."

21. Why did you leave your last position?

Keep this answer basic. In the event that you were laid off basically say as much, If your organization cut back, just say as much. Try not to go into a ton of subtle element. On the off chance that you were ended you will need to say you were let go however dependably catch up that accordingly you have figured out how to defeat this and feel it won't influence you later on.

22. What are your long range objectives?

The interviewer is trying to figure out whether or not you are going to be a long term employee or whether or not you will be using this job as a stepping stone to another objective. So, you should try to assure him/her that your intention is to stay with the company and to grow in your career within the company. You should respond "I am looking for a position with a company where I can stay and grow with and I feel this position would give me this opportunity."

23. What sort of machines or gear have you worked with?

This is your chance to give some point of interest of what genuine work abilities you have. Try not to be unclear, supply the majority of the data that you bring to the table.

24. What sort of compensation would you say you are searching for?

Try not to get into this subject unless you are compelled to. And still, after all that you need to leave a feeling that you are adaptable around there.

25. What do you think about our organization?

This is your chance to demonstrate to them that you have taken the time to research their organization specifically.

26. Do you have whatever other aptitudes of encounters that we have not examined?

Rundown all the required aptitudes for the position. You can likewise examine any leisure activities or volunteer experience you have and talk about any interest courses or instructive redesigning you have.

Chapter 10: What Not To Do

Don't Be Negative

Think of Good Weaknesses

Interviewers commonly ask, "What is your biggest weakness?" This is a tricky one as you don't really want to say you are not good at something, but you also don't want to appear arrogant by saying you are good at everything! Think of something that could be still be seen as a positive, or something that can easily be remedied, like "I tend to take on too much at once, but have learnt to delegate." This shows that you are helpful and not lazy and that you have learnt how to solve your weakness. For an in-depth look into how to turn your weaknesses into positive traits, take another look at this section.

Again, the recruiters are not interested in your weaknesses, but rather on how you deal with them and move forward. If you have a problem getting out of bed every morning, they don't want to know about it. What they are more interested in is, how you combat that bout of morning laziness and get to work on time. Be careful when talking about your negatives so as not to attach them to your performance at work.

Also, you might feel like it is a weakness but don't quote things like I trust people very easily, or I just can't help being there for everyone' or I work way too hard for my own good. It would come off as oblivious, unprofessional and disingenuous. Instead, state something like I am overly critical of myself or I attempt to please everyone.

The best way to answer this question is to spend little time on the weakness and more on how you combat it and let it help you move forward. Again, use the tactics mentioned above to jot down your weaknesses and how to effectively communicate them.

Sample Answer

Keywords: Insecurity, self-critical, lack of social skills, take matters too personally, presentation skills, excessively detail-oriented, lack of trust.

"I have a problem delegating tasks to other people for fear they might mess it up. I have spent sleepless nights in order to meet deadlines on time rather than assigning tasks to team members. I try to break the tasks into smaller milestones and conduct regular meetings to check for progress so as to ensure everyone's on the same page. I have realized checking up on progress frequently has helped me and my team members establish trust and meet deadlines in an efficient manner."

Don't Get Anxious

Obviously, as the interview is wrapping up, you're going to genuinely and authentically thank the interviewer (or interviewers) for their courtesy and for taking time out of their busy day to meet with you. Shake hands, look the interviewer(s) in the eye, use their name. (Mr. James, I appreciate your taking the time to see me today. I enjoyed meeting you and our conversation very much. Thank you so much for your kindness.)

When you're able to do so, compose and send an email from your computer (not your iPhone) reiterating your appreciation and asking them to please contact you if they have additional questions.

Keep the email short and sweet – if you promised to provide additional information following the interview (a sample of your work, perhaps) include it with this email.

Include your contact phone number and your email address and close the email politely.

Next, hand-write a Thank You note to each of the interviewers expressing your interest in the position and perhaps a mention of something the interviewer will recall from your meeting: I appreciate you taking the time to explain the water interchange process to me in detail. It really made the whole process much clearer to me.

The Thank You note itself should be a professional-grade note – nice stationery or card stock, perhaps with the words "Thank You" written or embossed on the front, but blank on the inside to hold your own handwritten notes. No silly picture Thank You cards from the drugstore. You can purchase a box of professional looking Thank You notes at a stationery or Hallmark store.

Use your best cursive handwriting. Address the envelope from the business card received from the interviewer, and double-check the interviewer's name (spelling) and address. Make sure you put a stamp on the envelope. (You wouldn't believe how many times people forget this tiny step) Drive immediately to a mail drop-off site and mail it. Don't wait two or three days to do this, because you'll never get it done.

A follow-up phone call after a few days is acceptable, but don't call every day, and definitely don't call multiple times in the same day. It's acceptable if you call once every other day for a week. If the individual doesn't pick up the phone when you call, simply leave a voicemail message for him/her, expressing your appreciation one last time.

The reason I recommend that you don't call multiple times in a single day is because, even if you don't reach the person 'live', the interviewer's phone shows them a record of all the phone numbers that have called. Don't look like a stalker with your phone number showing up 17 times in one day. Call once. If no answer, leave a message once.

Please look over the Bonus content following, to be completely ready for your interview. Best wishes for a successful and fruitful job hunt!

Why You Should Not Build a Second Personality

It is always easy to make a good result when you prepare for an interview, but what if you can't respond to an interview question even after a proper preparation?

1. Don't fake

Your inability to answer a question could be very embarrassing, but coming up with answers that you are unsure of is uncalled for. It is better to tell the interviewer in a very polite manner that you don't know the solution rather than creating solutions that don't relate to the question or sorry sounds senseless. You can eliminate some doubt by assuring your interviewer of carrying out some research or brooding more on the question.

2. Don't panic

Panicking when you can't answer an interview question is a big mistake and should be avoided. When you panic, your mind goes uncontrollable, and you get scared. Panicking is what you should avoid as it tends to ruin your whole interview performance. If you find it hard to answer an interview question, it means other candidates have the same issue too. So there is nothing to panic about.

3. Stay calm

When you find it difficult to answer an interview question, stay quiet as your reactions to a question are considered more important than your ability to answer it. Instead of reacting, maintain a relaxed and positive posture when faced with a difficult question.

4. Try to clarify

Clarification eliminated every possibility of misunderstanding the question. When you find a question difficult, try to locate the exact word that's confusing you. You can ask the interviewer to throw more light on the word or term confusing you, or you could ask for more explanation concerning the question.

The initial moments of an interview are all about assessing fit. Often unconsciously and before even discussing your experience and skills, an interviewer will be trying to determine if you have a "feel" that could work well for the position. He or she will be picking up on the personality signals you project. How do you carry yourself? How well would you align with the company's culture?

You want the interviewer to be internally saying yes right off the bat. Building rapport sets the tone and often impacts the types of questions you will be asked. Because everyone likes to be correct, if the first impression the interviewer has of you is positive, he or she will seek to prove that instinct right throughout the rest of the interview. The interviewer may even be more inclined to ask you questions that allow you to highlight strengths and shine, and to help you out if you get tripped up.

In short, people like to trust their first impressions. This phenomenon is often referred to as the halo effect: feeling generally good or bad about a candidate based on one thing heard or observed early during the interview, which then colors the evaluation of all the candidate's other attributes. If you establish a good rapport in the initial moments, chances are that your interviewer will carry this positive impression of you throughout the course of your meeting. Likewise, if you do something jarring or inappropriate that creates a negative first impression, this is the instinct that the interviewer will be inclined to trust, and you will have to work extra hard to reset the halo. The first five minutes of an interview are crucial for strengthening positive rapport.

Chapter 11: Get To There Early

The night before your job interview make sure to stay in and get yourself prepared for your interview, reviewing perhaps the question that you will ask your future boss. If your friends call and want you to go out drinking and socializing politely refuse and tell them you are staying in. Do not succumb to peer pressure because this could end up costing you the job you are interviewing for. You do not want to show up at your interview looking tired and hungover and smelling bad for your interview.

Don't Schedule Anything the Day Before Interview

You should try and take the day off before your interview or try not to schedule anything for that day. Instead spend that day getting yourself prepared for the interview on the following day. Make sure that your outfit that you are planning on wearing is not all full of wrinkles but is nice and pressed. Give it a nice around over the night before hanging it up nicely. Have the shoes that you are wearing for the interview nice and polished sitting under your suit. Make sure that you have set your alarm clock so that you can get up in plenty of time to shower before your interview and get yourself nice and well groomed.

Having a list of the things that you want to do in preparation for your interview is a good idea. Spend the morning of the interview going over your list and checking off what you have taken care of to be prepared for your interview. You want to give yourself enough time to prepare yourself so that you are going to show up at the interview early. Always show up early to an interview it shows that you are keen and are seriously interested in the position and are taking the interview seriously.

Use Google Map

You want to make sure that you will arrive for your interview at least half an hour early. You must take into consideration traffic jams. If you are not sure of the exact location of your interview it is a good idea to do a dry run there perhaps on the day before the interview. Have a look on Google map to get the directions to the location. It is best to do a dry run then you can time how long it takes you to get from where you live to the location of job. You do not want to show up to an interview late that is more than likely going to cost you your chance of getting the job. Showing up late to an interview is basically giving the future boss the message that you are not a dependable person.

Wash Your Hands Just Before the Interview

While you are sitting waiting to be called for your interview ask the secretary where the washroom is, then go there and wash your hands to prevent them from becoming sticky and sweaty. You do not want to offer you future boss a wet sticky hand, this will not be off to a good start, they will see this as you not being a confident individual. So make sure that you wash and dry your ends very thoroughly. Check your appearance and make sure all is looking good. Make any final adjustments to makeup or hair.

Dress up for Interview without Being Noticed by Your Current Boss

Many companies today allow their employees to dress business casual, or even allow them to wear jeans. You don't want to dress up in the morning making your current boss suspicious of what you may be up to. You might be better to take half the day or a full day off on the day of your interview. You could also drive somewhere perhaps home if you live close enough and change into the suit for your interview.

I think the best choice if you can is to take of that whole day so that you can get ready at home making sure you are dressed properly. You don't want to be dressing somewhere else and end up parts of your clothing are stuck in others, in the rush to get ready you missed this. Walking into an interview with your outfit out of whack could end up costing you that job. When you are getting ready in the comfort of your own home you can take the time to give yourself a good look over and make sure you look the part.

Chapter 12: Three Mistakes People Make During An Interview

Not enough confidence – For any job, any field, any industry one thing that an employer wants you to have is confidence. Having confidence does not mean walking into an interview acting like you already have the job and like you own the place. It simply means believing in yourself, your knowledge and your abilities. What you want to get across to the interviewer is that you can do the job. If you think about it there are two reasons that employers want to get out of an interview. Number 1 – Can you do the job? , Number 2 – Will you fit in with the rest of the team? If you can convince the employer of these two things you're in. When someone is lacking confidence and they are being interviewed it creates other problems that originally were not there, things such as being nervous, losing your train of thought and not giving the complete answer. When applying for a position you should know that you can do the job otherwise you will be setting yourself up for failure. This is the case with a lot of people but we'll leave this for another discussion. So, if you're already at the interview stage it means that you have passed the pre-screening process and that the employer obviously liked what they have seen regarding your education and experience which means that you have no reason not to be confident. Many people do not realize that getting the interview is a very big deal and should try not to be nervous and basically should just concentrate on expressing everything that they have on their resumes verbally. This should not be hard if you are really familiar with your resume and if you can think of really good examples of your past work experiences.

Too much confidence – I'll start off be repeating what I said under the first point "Having confidence does not mean walking into an interview acting like you already have the job and like you own the place. It simply means believing in yourself, your knowledge and your abilities.". Very large numbers of people believe that they are simply the best and that no one else compares to them, this most likely is NOT the case. People with too much confidence come across as being stubborn and usually are not liked by the employers because it makes the employer believe that if you are hired you will refuse certain jobs because you might think that you are above certain things and that you only deserve to do jobs that are considered to be high level. People that fall in this category are often thought of as not being team players and that they will be high maintenance employees because their expectations will be very high. This is something you do not want to do in an interview. Be confident but do not take it too far.

Not knowing enough about the position or the company – This might not make a lot of sense to people that are very organized in their job search and to those that keep track of every position that they apply to but it happens more than people realize. This is the one mistake that can be fixed without much effort; all it takes is some organization. Individuals that apply to a large number of positions often forget where they have applied, if they have sent an email, applied on-line through the company's website or if they simply gave their resume to a friend. Keeping track of your applications is very important. This is the reason a lot of people get confused about the specifics of a certain position and forget to do their research on the company. Employers love it when an applicant comes in and is able to discuss the specifics of a position and also to be able to talk about the direction their company is headed in. It is always a good idea to come to the interview with a few questions which ask about the position and the team that you would be working with as well as the growth possibility of the company and some of the major contracts that they are currently working on. Questions like this show the interviewer that you are genuinely interested in the position and the company since you have done a lot of research and are familiar with their work.

What to Do After the Interview

Finally, the interview is over and you have done everything you can to secure a job offer from that employer, right? Wrong, here are some tips on what to do after you leave the interview room:

Immediately following the interview, write down the interviewer's name (if you didn't obtain a business card) and your thoughts about the company and position – if you are interviewing for numerous jobs over a period of time, this technique will help you keep all of your job applications straight and provide you with a pro/con list if a job offer is extended

Send a Thank You note/email to the interviewer

If the employer falls behind on the hiring timeline that was discussed with you during the interview, follow up with a phone call to inquire about the status of the position

If you do not get the job, ask for some feedback from the employer so that you can be better prepared for the next job interview you obtain

Interview Do's & Don'ts:

Do maintain a positive, professional attitude

Do answer questions clearly and thoroughly – if you are unsure whether or not you have provided enough information, ask the employer if they require further clarification

Do demonstrate enthusiasm for the company, industry and position

Do conduct extensive research on the company and the industry before the interview

Do practice answering questions prior to the interview

Do prepare some questions in advance that you would like to ask the interviewer

Do maintain eye contact

Don't refer negatively to past employers or jobs – if an interviewer asks you share a negative experience, place emphasis on how you handled the situation and what you learned from it to develop effective coping mechanisms in the future

Don't arrive late for an interview – plan to arrive at least 15 minutes early

Don't talk in generalities – be specific about your skills and use concrete examples to back up your points

Don't slouch or sit with your arms firmly crossed - be aware of your body language and the unconscious messages you may be sending

Don't act chummy with the interviewer or tell jokes – instead, maintain a friendly, professional attitude

Don't dress casually for a job interview – make sure that your outfit is business-like so that you convey a professional image. Don't forget about your shoes – running shoes does not go with a suit!

Types of Interview Questions

In interviews that are considered to be structured there are typically two types of questions interviewers will use: behavioural questions and situational questions. Both types of questions are based on critical incidents that are required to perform the job but they differ in their focus.

Analyses have found mixed results for which type of question will best predict future job performance of an applicant. For example, some studies have shown that situational type questions have better predictability for job performance in interviews, while, other researchers have found that behavioral type questions are better at predicting future job performance of applicants. In actual interview settings it is not likely that the sole use of just one type of interview question is asked. A range of questions can add variety for both the interviewer and applicant. In addition, the use of high-quality questions, whether behavioral or situational based, is essential to make sure that candidates provide meaningful responses that lead to insight into their capability to perform on the job.

Behaviour Based Interviewing:

Behaviour based interviewing is a technique used by employers to learn about how you have behaved in past experiences in order to better predict how you will perform in their job. When answering this type of interview question, it is very important to refer to a specific situation and talk about what you did and how it turned out.

It is imperative that you practice for this type of interview, to allow yourself to become comfortable speaking about your past experiences as they relate to this job.

How to prepare for a behaviour based interview:

Review the job description and highlight the skills required to perform effectively in this position

For each skill required, think about 2 or 3 examples from your past educational, work or extra-curricular experiences of when you have demonstrated this skill

Practice speaking about each related experience – remember to explain:

The situation in which you demonstrated the skill

The challenges you faced in association with this experience

The actions you took in this situation

The end result or outcome of the experience

Sample Behaviour Based Questions:

Describe a situation when you were able to identify a conflict between two individuals and were instrumental in the solution to that conflict.

How do you behave when you encounter a problem with a co-worker?

Tell us about a time when you experienced a steep learning curve in a job. What did you do to learn all the material you needed to know?

How do you decide what gets top priority when scheduling your time?

Chapter 13: Face To Face Interviews

Just as in the phone interview it is important to dress the part. Be sure to look your absolute best and feel your best. No matter what type of interview you will have it is important to eat and sleep well to give your body and mind the fuel it needs to function at its absolute best. Appearing tired and haggard for an interview will tell the company that you are unorganized and therefore untrustworthy.

Leave for your interview well before the time it should begin. This will leave you an ample window should there be any roadblocks or accidents along the way. Arrive at least ten to fifteen minutes prior to your interview slot and check in letting them know you have arrived. Doing so will show the person with whom you are interviewing that you view them as important.

Bring a few copies of your resume for reference. This will allow anyone who may be joining in on the interview who has not seen your qualifications the ability to do so. This also demonstrates preparedness. Having a copy for yourself will also allow you to refer to your resume quickly should the need arise.

Just as in a phone interview, smiling when speaking will help convey your positivity. Send out positive energy with your initial greeting, giving a clear and firm handshake, and looking your interviewer in the eye. If you have more than one interviewer in the room be sure to greet each of them with the same smile and handshake.

With a face to face interview you may have an opportunity to know who you will be meeting. In this case take the time to research them. If you are able to make personal connections with your interviewer it will break the ice and make the process more enjoyable for both of you.

Study the job description and take note of any keywords which may be consistent through other listings similar to the position you are interviewing for and of course the actual listing for which you have applied. Prepare your stories and answers for your interview questions and incorporate these keywords into your response. Doing this will show the interviewer you have a firm concept of the themes and requirements to perform the job efficiently. The more keywords you have relationships and proven experience with will be more checked boxes for the needs and desires of the hiring executive.

Every interview is set up with a question and answer session. Some fields may require you to take a test of some kind to demonstrate your skill set however they should notify you if this is something which is required. Most interviews will consist of questions concerning certain scenarios such as explaining what you would do if something specific happened while on the job or how you would handle conflict resolution. Sometimes the questions will consist of you talking specifically about past projects and what you liked and didn't like about your previous or current position.

Supervisors who conduct interviews are looking for a person's ability to answer quickly with honesty and the person's personal set of values and how they tie in with the values of the company. Quick fire question and answer sessions allow an interviewee less time to think on their toes which will expose a person's more honest nature.

If an interviewer has thoroughly examined your resume they may ask more pointed questions towards your personal mission statement, lifetime goals, desires for the positions for which you are applying and history of the listed projects or positions you have provided. In that time it is always helpful to provide more details which may not be provided in writing which show your specific skill set and capabilities.

Usually near the end of the interview you will be provided time to ask them any questions you may have. Remember that an interview is not only for you. An interview is also for you to see if the company and the people you would be working with are a good fit for you. Ask questions which will give you a good idea if you could see yourself working in the position for an extended period of time. Do not be shy about asking questions. It is just as important to see if you feel at home with the company in question as they feel about hiring you.

If there is a longer process for interviewing, after your initial interview, you may find yourself with a few more interviews to follow. You may interview again with the same person or group you had interviewed with prior or it may be someone completely different. Do not feel bad about asking the same types of questions or answering and responding in the same manner as your previous interview. You may feel a bit like a broken record but it is important to stick to who you are. Chances are a new person interviewing you will have no previous knowledge on the types of answers you had provided in your initial interview.

While in your interview you should also pay attention to your posture. Are you sitting strait or are you hunched over? Do you cross your arms which gives off a defensive energy? Being open with your posture, confidant and sitting or standing tall will show that you are open to meeting new people and are able to communicate openly.

When you sit down to conduct your interview, try mirroring the posture, vocal cadence and body language of the person interviewing you. This does not mean you should copy them but try to match the speed at which they speak and the openness of their body language. Doing this will make the interviewer more comfortable with you. This is a tactic which uses similarities in body language and communication to to subconscious connect to the other person.

Use the "nuggets," technique which gives you small amounts of information that you can pick out about a person or a company. This can include the research you have conducted previously. It can also be positive comments towards your interviewer which compliment the interviewer or the company. Everyone loves to hear positive things about themselves and doing this can increase your chances of your interviewer warming up to you. Be careful about how much you use this technique, as doing too much of this can appear like you are reaching too much. Keep the compliments honest and sincere.

Be a good listener in your conversation and never interrupt. Always wait for a pause in the interviewer's speaking to move the conversation forward or respond. Also allow the interviewer to be the leader.

Remember that a first interview can be part of a larger scale screening process. There may be many other people they need to meet with before they can offer you a second interview. The goal of your face to face is to make yourself memorable and secure that second interview if the process calls for one.

Never speak of salary or benefits but be prepared to answer that question if it should come up as a question in your interview. Remain positive throughout your conversation and keep your eye on the prize. Remaining confident can help you take the needed steps forward. Now let's take a deeper look into the top questions you may be asked in your interview, why they are being asked, and what you can avoid to make your interview top notch.

SECOND INTERVIEWS

Being invited to a second interview means you have made it to the next stage in the hiring process! This means you have been invited with a handful of other candidates for the final stages of the hiring process and are one of a few people who are still in the running for the position. In a second interview you have a higher chance of interviewing with your potential boss if you have not already. You could also be interviewing with multiple people or perhaps another supervisor higher up. Your interview could also be with the hiring manager for a second time or the human resources representative.

Less likely, but possible, you could be meeting with possible members of your team in a group interview process. The members of the team could be sitting down with you to ask you questions to see if you would be a good fit within the already existing team dynamic. You could also be interviewing with a high-level or member of executive leadership.

Your second interview will give you a deeper insight into the job itself. It should answer any detailed questions you may have and you should understand the company, leadership team, group dynamic, and projects you will be working on with more clarity. The interview will more often than not focus on how the day to day operations work in the position.

Within this interview your interviewer will also focus on more detailed aspects of why you are the strongest candidate for the position. Do not be surprised if your questions lean more towards the negative aspects of your last position. In this case do continue to remain positive in your answers and work towards turning the conversation to how you have continued to grow and learn within your position.

Prepare for your second interview by reviewing your notes from your first interviews. You may have had many conversations with the hiring manager, human resources, your potential boss, or even other employees. Carefully read through those notes and information you have to help you feel more prepared and gain a deeper in depth look at the company and position itself.

Doing this will help you search for more questions you may have that you have not yet asked. This review will also refresh your memory regarding the company and the discussions you have already had. Also review the job posting and refresh your knowledge of the position and its requirements and what the position requires.

Practice once again the common interview questions and your responses to these questions. Your second interview may feel a bit like a repeat of your first interview, but regardless of whom you are speaking with, do your best to act as though it is your first time meeting your interviewer and this is the first time you are answering these particular questions.

After all of your interviews it is a nice gesture to send thank you notes to your interviewers. Thank them for their time and express your gratitude for their time. Do not wait to send these thank you letters but instead send them immediately. Do your best to add in specifics about your conversation to show that you were actively and genuinely engaged in the conversation. Restate your interest in the position and thank them for giving you the opportunity to meet them and learn more about what the company has to offer.

Chapter 14: Education Questions

While your curriculum vitae or resume provides the interviewer with an overview of your career and education, it is impossible for it to provide all the minor details that they would want to know. So, they would prefer to fish those out from you during the interview. Therefore, it is imperative for you to master your entire professional and academic background like it is the back of your hand. That way, you can answer all of these questions with complete confidence in your abilities, knowledge, and experience.

What was it like working as a...?

Before walking into the interview, be prepared to describe the details of your responsibilities during your current or previous job. Take care not to be too particular about the insignificant parts, because the interviewer might just get bored. Instead, highlight between three and five important roles that you played and which are related to the position you are applying for.

As a Marketing Assistant of Company ABC, I was responsible for social media marketing. Specifically, I had three main roles. First was to constantly update all the social media accounts of ABC on a regular basis, so that we would regularly be trending on our target market's feeds. Second was to create innovative promotions for our latest products and to collaborate with the marketing director for fresh ideas that we can launch on social media. Third was to communicate with our online subscribers and to ensure that all the queries and concerns they post on our social media sites are handled immediately.

What are you most proud of having achieved in your career so far?

Your response should reflect something your interviewer can relate to, not something that's so industry-specific it only applies in the matchbook printing industry, and you're interviewing for a position in management consulting. Broaden your thought process, know this question will come, and be prepared with several possible responses, from which you can select the one most likely to be seen by someone in the job for which you're interviewing. I had the opportunity to become Green Belt Six Sigma Certified in my current role, and the tools and methodologies I learned have enabled me to really shine when it comes to data analysis.

What professional certifications or licenses do you hold? How long have you had them? What are the requirements for maintaining or renewing them?

The interviewer wants to make sure you're committed to any professional certifications or licenses you've taken the time to attain. Most certifications or licenses will require that you take exams or classes, or attend seminars to stay current with trends in your industry or specialized expertise area. I'm certified as a Microsoft Certified Solutions Associate (MCSA) and a Microsoft Certified Solutions Expert (MCSE). I get recertified every three years, and recertification requires taking an exam. My last recertification exam was in August of last year and my score on the exam was 98%.

What do you dislike about your job?

By asking this, what the interviewer really wants to know is if there is anything that might potentially cause you to leave their company in case they do hire you. It also helps the interviewer understand one of the reasons why you are looking for a new job.

One thing to remember is that you must not say that there is no aspect of your previous or current job that you do not like. Otherwise they would question why you are even applying for a new one in the first place.

Instead, be ready to answer this by considering aspects of the job which you do not like but which are out of your own control. Just make sure that these same aspects are not present in the organization you are applying to. Then, make sure that you choose your words carefully and not sound as if you hate your previous or current job. End on a positive note, such as by highlighting what you like in their organization that is not offered in the previous one.

In my previous work, I was required to visit all the factories in the entire country, so I spent most of my week traveling. It was quite exciting at first, but now I am highly considering a position where I can spend more of my productive hours working instead of being on the road. This is one of the reasons why I am attracted to this position you are offering.

What did you enjoy most about elementary school? High school? College? Post-grad?

They've already learned about who you are and what your background is, but they still want to get to know who you really are. We all have experiences that helped to identify us, but it is our emotions, feelings, and reactions that really help to make up the person that we are. They will likely ask what you liked most about school, so be honest!

When I was in school, I used to love science classes. I was always curious about the way the world worked. As I made my way into high school, I focused more on arts and expressing myself. When I entered college, I started to really be more interested in the community that surrounded me and how I could actually affect the people in the community.

Why did you stop working for each of these companies?

The interview wants to know what causes you to stop working at each company as it is a glimpse of the kind of person you are. They are also concerned about their attrition rate, or the number of people who leave because of certain reasons. This question is commonly asked if your CV shows how you have many jobs but did not stay more than a year and a half in most, if not all, of them.

The right way to answer this question is to provide an acceptable, positive reason. Never say anything negative about your previous job unless you are required to do so.

Some of the most widely accepted reasons for leaving are: greater security or stability at work, wanting bigger challenges or responsibilities, and seeking a full-time position.

While I truly enjoyed my past 12 months with Company X, I have become increasingly drawn towards projects that are more creative and challenging. Unfortunately, the head manager wanted the team to follow the exact same video-editing style in every project. This is the main reason why I want to become a part of your organization as I have heard that you want each project to be completely unique each time.

Would you call yourself a good manager?

If the position will require you to manage others or work with a team, then the interviewer will highly likely as this question. Of course, do not end by simply saying, Definitely! or Yes, indeed! Instead, elaborate on the why. Specifically, the interviewer wants to hear you mention between three to five managerial skills that will shed light on your experiences in management.

To help you shape your own answers out, here are some of the key phrases that interviewers would love to hear from you: delegating and supervising tasks, coaching or mentoring team members, motivating the team, collaborating with the board and team, and creating different strategies for the team.

Yes, and I believe my team will agree with me. My role as the manager was to collaborate with both the team and the board to create new strategies for our business. After that, I worked on delegating tasks to those who were best fit for the requirements. Throughout every project, I not only supervised but also provided both group and one-on-one mentoring sessions with the team members regularly. I am proud to say we were able to deliver and satisfy our clients within schedule every time.

What can you say about your previous/current company?

No matter how tempting it might seem, you should never say anything bad about the company you are currently work – or you previously worked – for. This will only make you look like a difficult employee. On the other hand, praising it too much might make them think why you would even consider leaving.

Instead, what you can do is to strike a balance by mentioning both the strengths and weaknesses of the company. Then, mention the best factors of the company you are applying to and why you find yourself with them in the near future.

My previous/current company has a wonderful work environment, especially since the managers made sure that we were constantly coached and updated with the latest updates in the industry. On the other hand, it has not expanded in the last five years, leaving me with no opportunity to grow. This is why I am eager to become a part of your organization, because my research showed that you are fast-growing and dynamic.

May we contact those on your reference list?

The best way to respond to this would be to request the interviewers to hold off from contacting those on your reference list until you have received a job offer. The main reason is so that you would not want your previous employer's office to have to answer so many calls from the organizations you have applied to. However, if you have already mentioned to your previous employer that you would like them to be in your references list, then you can go ahead and say yes to the interviewer.

On the other hand, if you are still with the company that is in your references list, then you need to carefully explain to the interviewer that you are concerned about alarming your current company that you are applying to another company.

I'd be delighted for you to give them a call later on and I am certain that they will provide you with supporting evidence of what I have mentioned in this interview. But would it be alright if it would be postponed until you have decided to make me an offer? I would not want to draw attention from them about my looking for a position in your company.

Chapter 15: What You Will Bring To The Position

Once they have gotten what a sense of your personality is like, they will then start to try and investigate why they should pick you over all the other candidates. You made it past the point of being a qualified person on an individual level through your own character and experiences. This is your chance to shine and set yourself apart from all other candidates.

Remember to not simply memorize the answers that we are giving you. This only makes it harder on you in the actual interview. The point of the example answer is just so you can get a sense of a realistic and solid response. Keep it personalized to you, because setting yourself apart from the rest is of utmost importance!

"Tell me where you see yourself in the future (six months/five years/ten years from now)."

This is a common question that interviewers might even ask right at the beginning of the interview. This is a question that will be inclusive of all aspects of your life. Where do you see yourself in your career? What about your family life? In your personal goals? They don't just want to hear, "Hopefully working here!" They want to know that you are thinking about your future and that you have a plan. They want to see if they will fit into your plan. You might consider saying something like this when that question is asked:

"In six months, I hope that I am settled into a position and in a place where I can focus on really improving my skills. At the same time, I want to ensure that I'm doing my best to also consistently check in with my personal goals. Eventually, I hope to achieve a position of employment where I'm making a comfortable amount of money. I know the future is always changing so I'm also excited to see what surprises the future might bring me!"

"Why should we hire YOU?"

Every job will have several people applying for the position. All of the questions asked so far likely helped them to realize whether or not they want to hire you based on your experience and so on, but other candidates have probably fit the criteria they have too. Why should they hire you and not someone else? What stands out about you that will make you the best candidate? This is going to be specific to you. Perhaps you have a valuable skill that's hard to come by. Maybe it's something in your history that makes you unique. What are the qualities that really set you apart from the competition?

"I believe I'm the right pick because of my set of skills and experiences that I have had. I not only do what I'm asked, but I make sure to go above and beyond and deliver something greater than what I was asked. I take pride in my work, even if it is not a task I am particularly passionate about at the moment. I will always deliver work with exceptional detail and attention to the things that matter the most."

"What about this position makes you want to work here? Why do you want to get hired?"

The "Why do you want to work here" question is always going to be in the interview. It's not a trick question! Your interviewer will legitimately want to know why it is that you chose them. The obvious answer is, "Because I need a job and I saw you were hiring. I want money." This is usually the first thing that we will consider when applying to a job. While this might be the truth, try to honestly remember why it is that you want this position and not another. Have your reason prepared before even making your way into the interview. When you can give substantial answers based directly on their mission statement, then that will give you a big advantage.

"I want to work here because I have always been a lifelong supporter of this company. I have frequented the stores and I understand what the clientele is like. Not only do I think this will help me to be more passionate and dedicated to my work, but I think it helps because I will be more knowledgeable about what the business actually stands for. When I have this connection to the workplace, it is easier to go above and beyond because I have the confidence to know what my talents are and how the company will benefit from them."

"What do you know about us? How would you describe our company?"

This is a question that will require a lot of research! Make sure you Google your company before the interview. Don't just go to their site either. Read reviews if it is a service-based place or a retail location. If it is a huge company, look up news articles that might focus on them. Go on forums and see if anyone else has worked there and what their stories are like. The more you know about them, the easier this will be. Make sure that you list out what their services are, what their employees do, and what their mission statement is. This is a specific question, so make sure that your answer is based specifically on the company that you are interviewing for!

"What unique skills do you have that only apply to this specific position?"

This is another specific one that will apply only to the position that you are interviewing for. If you are looking to get hired as a front desk clerk, then you would want skills involving talking to people, handling requests, taking messages, making appointments, and other clerical work. If you are applying to be a construction worker, then you'll need to make sure that you can lift heavy things, operate heavy machinery, and have basic construction knowledge.

Whenever you are applying for a job, they'll usually have a list of objectives in their job description. Make sure that you study these. They will give you the exact insight needed to understand what unique skills that you have specifically for this job. They might have a job description that says things like:

Must be proficient in Word

Have excellent communication skills

Punctual and reliable

And so on.

Remember them, and when you get to your interview, you will be able to state them in your own way. Discuss your technical skills on the computer. Talk about how you can communicate. Give examples of how you are reliable. When you bring up keywords that they're looking for, they're going to be more likely to keep you in the back of their mind when making the final decision.

"What are you hoping to accomplish in this position?"

This is a seemingly obvious question, but it can actually catch a lot of people off guard. It seems to be one of the most obvious questions that can actually reveal a deeper truth about someone who might be applying for the job. There are a few ways that you can answer this. You can discuss how you would like to move up to a higher position if that is something you believe to be an option. Alternatively, you can discuss how you hope to gain valuable skills if it is not a position that offers a lot of growth.

"I hope while I'm working here, if hired, of course, that I can discover new skills that I may have and improve on things I need to work on while also helping the business thrive. I know the things that I need to improve on, and I have goals for myself. I think this company's goals and the goals I have for myself line up well together so that we can both mutually benefit from what I might experience here."

"How many responsibilities do you feel comfortable having at a time?"

This is a good question to help them to determine whether or not you are a multi-tasker. Some people are comfortable handling just one thing at a time, while others can handle several different things at once. Do your best to answer honestly because even if you struggle to do several things at once, that doesn't mean you're not a good employee! We all have a different pace for completing tasks so ensure that you are being honest with them. Can you handle several projects, or are you someone that works at a slower pace on one thing at a time? While you can easily lie and say that you can take on a bunch of things at once, you are just setting yourself up to make things more challenging later on. Be honest!

"I am pretty good with time management, so I don't mind taking on a few things at once. I will always try to complete tasks much faster than I say I will so that I can go above and beyond. I don't take on too much at once because I know my limits and do my best to avoid feeling overwhelmed or burnt out."

"Can you adjust quickly to a rapidly changing environment? Would you be able to change your plans if something unexpected happened?"

There may be a time when your employer has to send you to a different location, or perhaps they need you to work in a different department, depending on your skills and the versatility of management. It is up to you, then, to make sure that you know how to adapt should a situation like this occur. Be honest with them and let them know if you are going to be able to quickly adapt to situations like this if that's what you have to do later on.

"I have no problem trying new things. I appreciate having a set schedule so that I know what needs to be done, but when things change, it can just make work feel more exciting, making going to work more enjoyable. I'm not concerned about my abilities to adapt should there be a situation when I need to quickly adjust to change."

"What strong organizational skills do you have?"

Being organized is incredibly important. They can simply ask, do you have this skill, or this skill, or this skill, and so on, but instead, they are leaving this question for you to fill in the blanks. Rather than blatantly stating that you are detail oriented, punctual, and so on, put an emphasis on sharing your actual steps to become organized so that they can have a better sense of whether or not you are really someone with a great set of organization skills.

"I think organization is incredibly important in order to avoid any issues that might arise during any given project. To get organized, I first make a list of all the tasks that I need to do. From there, I will prioritize them by importance and separate them by how much time they will take and look at ways that I might be able to complete two tasks simultaneously. From there, I do my best to adhere to timelines, always giving myself a little extra time to account for any incidents that might occur!"

"If you were part of a group project, and you started to feel as though other members weren't pulling their weight, how would you handle this situation?"

This can be a frustrating feeling. Maybe there's a group project that includes five people, but there's that one guy who is not pulling his weight. Alternatively, perhaps everyone else is doing all the work and not letting you have the chance to thrive. Your interviewer wants to know how you would handle it if you found yourself in either of these scenarios.

"First, I would address whether there are issues within myself. Am I not delegating tasks properly? Is there a lack of communication? I would ensure I was doing everything I could on my part, and then address issues within the group. I would do it one on one and pull people aside to have personal conversations about the project. If I felt like I wasn't having the opportunity to pull my weight and others were too controlling or were doing the work for me, I would take the same steps."

"What is a strong value that you have that is only related to a working environment?"

When we think of values, we might first think of religion, politics, or philosophy. You won't need to think of this for a question about your working values, however. They want to know what is important to you. How would you describe your work ethic? What is something that you always remind yourself when the going gets tough at work? This is another question specific to you, and there are a few ways you can answer. Here is one of them:

"One value that's important to me is persistence. Sometimes things don't go as planned, and you might have moments of failure, but I always remind myself to try again. If something consistently is not working, then I'll look for a different way to solve the problem. The more I focus on getting back on my feet and continuing the fight, the easier it is to achieve my goals. Even if I fail nine times, the 10th time might be the time I succeed, so it's always important for me to continue on."

"What traits do you think an employee in this specific position should have?"

This is an important question because it will be specific to the employees and what you know about the company already. It shows them what you really think that you will be doing in the position if hired. The question is not just about you, it's about the position. You should put yourself in the perspective of the person conducting the interview, making it easier to see what they might be looking for. When you can do this, it becomes easier to know what a good answer would be. You might base this on a job description that you saw, or it could simply be something that you gathered as you discussed different things throughout the interview. Your response might be something like this:

"I think that it's important for an employee in this position to be reliable. There are several people depending on them, and it seems as though there will be some high-pressure scenarios. If they can't be trusted professionally and personally, then that can put a wedge in the working environment."

"Can you sell me the chair that you are sitting on at the moment?"

This is a question that might be specific to those who are interviewing for a sales position. Even if you won't be working with sales, numbers, or customers at all, it can still be a question that pops up. It is one that will show how well you can try and persuade someone. Are you a good schmoozer? Do you have a creative mindset that helps you to see the benefits even in something as mundane as a chair?

They will ask questions like this especially if you are in sales, but the question might differ in how it is presented. They might say something like, "Sell me this pencil", or ask you to sell another object that's around. Your sales pitch might look like this:

"This chair is great for anyone who is looking to sit down. We all could use a break, and when we do decide to get that moment of rest, then this chair is going to be your top choice. It has a cushioned top that makes it comfortable for your bottom, especially for those sitting for long periods of time. It has features where you can adjust the height of the chair, so anyone can benefit from it. Not only does it have great comfort features, but it's aesthetically pleasing as well. Why don't you give it a try for yourself?"

"Is it more important for people to like you in a managerial position, or for people to fear you?"

This is a common question, especially if you are going to be interviewing for a managerial position. It's a frequent discussion of whether or not a manager is supposed to be feared or if they should be liked. Do you want to be the boss that's popular with everyone or is it more important that they become obedient and respect your authority? The best way to answer this is that you should be right in the middle of both.

Chapter 16: How To Grow In Your Career While Working Towards Your Dream Job

You must learn to be patient and know that you can't always get what you want when you want it such as your dream job. But while you are working towards it you can do things to improve your life inside and outside the job you are in at the moment.

1) **Your career is one important component of your life** but there are

other areas in your life that are just as important if not more so that you also need to pay attention to.

- Self (physical, emotional)
- Spiritual
- Finances
- Friends & Family

When you are doing well in all of these areas of your life you will be able to find more energy to focus towards your career goals.

2) **Stay focused on your future** don't spend time getting down and depressed at what is going on in your life at this point in time. You need to make a plan and have a goal giving yourself something to work towards accomplishing. It does not have to be a clear goal that you have in mind but at least a goal will help you to move forward. Your goal may change through time as well as your choice of career. But the important thing is that you are

3) **Long term view of your career.** It may take you a couple of years to get to where you want to be but won't it be great to be working at your dream job for the rest of your remaining career!

4) **Grateful Journal.** You should try and write down at the end of the night just before bed all things in your life that you are grateful this exercise will help you to focus.

5) **Think Positive.** During times such as your lunch break or when you are doing your daily exercise listen to uplifting podcasts. Michael Hyatt and Dan Miller are two that I would recommend. Choose positive reading material as well.

By using even some of the suggestions in this chapter they will help you to stay focused on the big picture of eventually getting to work at your dream job but also how to enjoy where you are at. Being thankful for what you do have in your life that is positive is very important in helping you to stay in a healthy state of mind instead of feeling down and depressed about your life. You must be patient and realize all your dreams cannot happen overnight but eventually through hard work and focusing on your goals you will get to where you want to be career wise. Learning to have some self discipline is good to help you stay on track do not get led away from your dream by some bad influences you must stay strong and move towards the light not away from it!

Choosing Your Next Career Move

Often people are so busy trying to package themselves to suit how the outside world perceives them that they forget who they really are and what they are all about. Deep down they know what they really want to do and be but many are afraid to take that step outside of the box so to speak that they have been stuck and labeled in.

How to Fix This. You must be in tune with the parts of you that are wonderful and the parts of you that need some work. If you embrace the real you it will enable you to find a higher level of success as a result. The more you understand where and how you shine the better equipped you will be to choose the next career move that will get you closer to your dream career.

Things You Can Do to Get to Know Yourself Better.

1) You can take a personality assessment.

2) Answer these questions about yourself

• What activities in your life have the greatest value?

• What do you see yourself doing when you daydream?

• List five phrases or words that best describe you

3) Do things that excite and energize you more.

4) Observe Yourself- write down what you think will happen as the result of a key decision you have made.

5) Find out what your strengths are and your weaknesses.

6) Write a personal journal

7) Ask friends and family how you come across in certain situations.

8) Identify what you truly value in life.

Chapter 17: What To Do When You Get There?

The moment you receive a call from an employer, you will get excited because you may have gotten the opportunity to fill the position available. Job applicants for the second or third time still get nervous as they are still not so confident about themselves. There are job applicants who need so much self-confidence and need to be relaxed before their scheduled interview.

This is your chance to get the job!

You are looking good and you have saved enough confidence and strength to go into your interview. All you need to do is **relax, believe in yourself** and follow these simple tips when you get to your scheduled interview!

Smile – this is the first thing you should give the people around the room when you walk in. A smile generates positive energy. It is the best thing to do anytime of the day; more so, for your interview. Getting into that room with a frown on your face will not help you at all. The interviewer might notice you for the negative thoughts you are sending out. Who would want an employee generating negative energy to the company? A simple smile will always go a long way in any situation. It is a simple gesture that leads you to a thousand miles in your new career. Just give them a smile and you are sure to give them a lasting good impression.

Answer clearly – no company needs an employee who stutters even on a simple question. It shows a lack of confidence. What significant things can you do for the company if you are hesitant at your first interview? It gives them a negative impression of you and they can lose interest in giving you a call back for a second interview. Just answer clearly and everything follows smoothly.

Ask questions – job applications also go with the times. Job applicants in the earlier years were not allowed to ask questions. You are a part of the modern job application system where you are allowed to ask some questions. Yes, you are given the privilege to do so in order for you to get a feel for the position and company you are applying for. In return, policies and rules together with benefits are laid down on the table for clearer understanding of what you can expect from the company.

Just sit down when not yet called – roaming around the room or going to and from the interviewer's table to check if it is already your turn is not the proper way to behave. Just sit down and don't worry as your name will be called at the soonest possible time. You will be advised at once when your interview is rescheduled. Sitting in place makes you alert of what is happening.

Chapter 18: Getting To The Venue

You have done your homework, made yourself presentable, and now it is time to face the music! This could easily be the most ignored aspect of a job interview. Many if not most people are so focused on preparing for the questions, perfecting their handshakes and their smiles that they miss out on time after leaving the house and before the interview. You will not only be judged based on your answers during the interview; you will be assessed on your temperament during the waiting period and your behavior towards other candidates and the staff in general. All these gestures and actions matter when the company is looking for someone to adjust within the corporation. Following are a few factors that you should keep in mind to give off a good impression about punctuality, mannerisms, and common etiquettes.

Check the Location Beforehand

The HR person getting in touch with you would likely send in directions to the place of the interview. You may have a good idea where it is, but if you don't travel to that part of the town often, then there is a fair chance you wouldn't know how long it would take to get there. Factors like traffic conditions, commute timings, and the exact location of the place could really affect the time it would take to get there. Technological advancements have eliminated the need to visit the premises physically. You can check the location on Google maps. You can also check the best routes, traffic conditions, and the estimated time it would take to get there. Even with all that information at your arsenal, keep a good ten minutes margin for any unexpected delays. Keep an additional 20 minutes of the interview is during rush hours. Also, if you are applying to a large corporation, then it may take some time to figure out where the said building or office is. What floor you need to head to and where the elevators are. It'd help to speak to the person getting in touch with you about the interview about the premises. But even then, add a few minutes more to be on the safe side.

Put Extra Money in the Parking Meter

Having extra money in the meter would just silent the clock ticking in your head. You want to be able to relax during the interview rather than keep checking the clock to see if the meter has run out.

Be on Time

Many times, arriving on time means any time before the interview, even if it means getting there an hour in advance! A good rule of thumb is to arrive 15 minutes before the appointed time, not earlier and definitely no later than the actual time. While arriving late could show carelessness, arriving much earlier in advance might leave a bad impression too. Say the staff is getting ready for the interview and you arrive an hour in advance. It would just make everyone a little uncomfortable. And all that wait would not do your nerves or your energy levels any favors either. On the other hand, you may have a pretty genuine excuse about how you had lost your key on the way to the venue as an excuse for running late; you will not be spared for it.

Checking In

When you arrive at the venue, you may need to check in at the reception. Even if you aren't asked to, don't just go sit with the other candidates assuming everything is in its place. Introduce yourself at the reception with your name, why you are there, what time you were expected to come and what position you are applying for. Here's an example: **"Hello, my name is Jessica Taylor. I am here for the 11 am job interview for the position of a project manager."** You may then be asked to wait a while. If someone comes to greet you, stand up, and shake their hands. Introduce yourself again. If you have spoken to them on the phone before, let them know it's nice to meet them in person. Be friendly, smile often, and remain confident.

Be Ready to Wait

The chances are you aren't the only person for the interview, so be ready to wait. Nerves and anxiety might make you feel like the interviewer has a personal vendetta against you, but he just has a lot of people to interview, and he would prefer being thorough with each and every one of them. Following are a few things to avoid when waiting for your turn:

Avoid checking the clock too much. It just shows you are impatient or perhaps have other 'more important matters' to take care of.

Avoid asking the staff how long it'd take. Put your phone on silent. Avoid playing on your phone or excessive texting and smiling. If you really want to calm your nerves by playing a game or a personality quiz, but don't let everyone else become a part of it through your gestures or game sounds.

Avoid moving around too much. You can go for a little walk, or to get some water or a trip to the loo, but don't go back and forth too much. It would just grab a lot of unnecessary attention.

Use the time to do a little search through the walls. Most companies have their accomplishments, their values, and goals pasted on the walls. This is a good time to learn a little more or get a reminder of the core values and culture of the company.

Be Courteous to Everyone Around

Don't treat the other candidates as a competition. You have made your preparations and have a game plan ready. Be confident in your own skills and talents and rather use their presence to make your own mark as a courteous, well-behaved individual. Stay relaxed and hold small talks with the people sitting close to you. Smile at them and ask for general information about them. However, do not talk about their qualifications or previous job or any other information related to them applying for this job. Also avoid talking about other taboo topics like religion, politics, finances, etc. Don't bring your personal problems with you either. They don't need to know about a family member's illness or your kid's deteriorating grades. All this just makes everyone unnecessarily uncomfortable and adds added pressure on already wrecking nerves. Smile at people and wish them good luck while they go in for the interview, you surely would want the gesture reciprocated when your turn comes.

Chapter 19: Presentation - Solution

You've built rapport. You've confirmed or uncovered the fear or dream that is motivating each interviewer. Now it's time to seize the moment.

You might still be in the question and answer portion of the interview. So you will still have to answer their questions in a thoughtful, smart manner. But now you are no longer trying to learn or get information from them.

Everything you say from this point forward should highlight the fact that you are the solution to their felt need.

If their felt need is a fear, everything should communicate that if they hire you, they do not have to fear. If their felt need is a dream then everything you communicate should play into that dream.

Do not lose focus. It can be very easy to get off topic or ramble about something that doesn't matter.

The main thing is the main thing.

Explode passion.

It has also been said that sales is all about transferring passion from the seller to the buyer. Don't be afraid to have a volcanic eruption of passion when talking about how your features provide a benefit that directly answers their fears or dreams. In fact you should have a volcanic eruption of passion. They might think you are strange and exuberant, but they will remember the feeling of how you spoke directly to their fears and dreams.

In the classic book on sales "How I Raised Myself From Failure to Success in Selling", Frank Bettger describes a time early in his sales career when he was ready to give up as an insurance salesman. Following the advice of a sales manager, who claimed he didn't show enough enthusiasm in his presentations, Bettger decided to give it one last try. In his next meeting he resolved to be nothing if not passionate about the insurance policy he was selling. He yelled and made big hand gestures and even pounded his fist on the prospective buyer's desk a number of times. At the end of the presentation he looked at the prospect expecting to get a disgusted rejection, but the prospect simply said "Ok, I'll buy from you."

People want to feel excited.

Nobody wants a boring existence and nobody wants a mundane, difficult job. When we see excited salespeople there is a subconscious thought that if we buy the product it will cause us to feel the same way.

In the job interview if you seem excited and even remotely capable of solving the interviewer's felt need then they begin to think about that need. They think about you solving it and this makes them excited too. And then they begin to look for reasons to justify hiring you. You have now turned them into an advocate for you.

If you have found the interviewers' felt needs, then be confident and speak passionately about how you solve that exact problem. You don't have to be eloquent. You don't have to be perfect. What you do have to be is enthusiastic and passionate about solving that need.

Chapter 20: Tips For Telephone Interviews

It can be very challenging to give a telephonic interview. The responses of the interviewer are not available, and this makes it difficult to gauge as to what the interviewer is expecting from you. This is exactly the reason why we are discussing this topic separately. This section provides some useful tips on handling telephonic interviews.

Voice is Important

Pay attention to how you answer the phone.

Be aware of flat, monotone responses.

Consider the recruiter sitting across you and answer as if they are present.

Show Enthusiasm and Interest

Although the employer can't see you, smile. Smile has an unconscious effect on your mind and body. It allows you to feel enthusiastic and energetic, and the same is conveyed in your conversations.

Listen Carefully!

Listen to the questions presented in an attentive manner and ask for clarification if needed

Ensure That Your Device Is In Perfect Condition And Speak Clearly

Do not consume, mull over gum, or smoke while, on the telephone, sound is intensified!

Do not keep the mouthpiece too close or away from the mouth. Ideally, the mouthpiece should be a distance of one inch from your mouth.

Do not utilize a speakerphone, regardless of the fact that the questioner does.

Look For A Calm Place For Talking

Be mindful that the questioner might really incorporate a gathering of individuals. In the event that they don't present themselves, inquire as to whether they would see any problems with doing so. Record their names and titles, and don't hesitate to ask who is inquiring as to whether you are not certain.

Positives Of Giving telephonic Interviews

Telephonic Interviews are not totally bad. They allow you flexibilities that face-to-face interviews can never give.

You can dress coolly.

You can chat with your hands.

You can utilize notes.

You can undoubtedly take notes. Keep paper and a pen by the telephone.

You can without much of a stretch allude to your resume, presentation document, and set of responsibilities.

Phone Etiquette

When your professional interactions involve the telephone, you must be aware of phone etiquettes and what can be destructive for you and your prospective career in the organization. Here are a few things that you must remember:

If an executive calendars a particular time to call you, verify you are accessible and that you have a calm spot to talk.

If you leave a message in the wake of giving back a missed call, dependably leave your first and last name, your telephone number and a decent time to get back to you.

Never put the management on hold while you reply "call holding up" or an alternate "approaching call."

If you have an incoming call while you are speaking to an executive, approach the executive to hold for a minute and pull it together. Don't put the employer on hold for more than 30 seconds. On the off chance that the timing is amazingly terrible for you, inquire as to whether you can furnish a proportional payback. Tell the boss the careful time that you will call, or organize a proper time advantageous to both of you and stick to that time.

Chapter 21: Ask Questions

Asking questions at the end of your interviews is in fact as important as answering them, it reinforces your suitability as a candidate and also provide you with a good opportunity to understand more about the role you are applying as well as the company you are applying to.

So you have scored that interview, made a great first impression, answered every question that came at you to perfection and built a good rapport with the interviewers. Then the interviewers ask if you have any questions for them. This is where you can demonstrate that you have truly given this role some serious considerations but posting a few insightful questions of your own. This will also help to leave a final good impression of yourself for the interviewers.

If you are still on the fence about joining, you should ask questions that are specific to what you want to find out. If you already have your mind set on getting hired, then then the questions you ask should reflect that you deserve to working for the company, as well as show that you are willing to move the company forward. Here are some great questions you can ask the company:

What have you enjoyed most about working here? This question allows the interviewer to connect with you on a more personal level, sharing his or her feelings. The answer will also give you an unique insight into whether the employees are happy working for that company. Employee satisfaction should play an important part in your decision making process. If the interviewer is pained to come up with an answer to your question, it may signal a red flag.

What skills and experiences would make an ideal candidate? This is a great question that will have the interviewer put his or her cards on the table and state exactly what the employer is looking for. If the interviewer mentions something you didn't cover yet, now is your chance.

What is the working environment like? If you have not talked about this in the interview proper, now is a great time to ask it. This question allows you to better understanding if you will truly enjoy working in the environment and also to find out about the working dynamics of the teams you will be working with.

Is there anything that I can help in the moment that I join? This question clearly shows that you are keen to be part of the team and want to offer your services right away. You can also ask the interviewer if you will be given the opportunity to develop breadth-wise in the company.

Can employees develop quickly in the company? This question is important of you want to find out about the possible career progression for yourself after joining the company. It also shows the interviewer that given the chance, you are committed to learning and developing yourself at the company for the long term.

Who previously held this position? This seemingly straightforward question will tell you whether that person was promoted or fired or if he/she quit or retired. That, in turn, will provide a clue to whether: there's a chance for advancement, employees are unhappy, the place is in turmoil or the employer has workers around your age.

What is the next step in the process? This is the essential last question and one you should definitely ask. It shows that you're interested in moving along in the process and invites the interviewer to tell you how many people are in the running for the position.

As you can see, asking questions will not only provide you with useful information but also help you differentiate yourself from the other candidates that are also applying to the similar role you are.

Chapter 22: Questions You Should Be Prepared To Answer At Job Interview

No matter how many you go on, job interviews can always be nerve-wracking. You put on your nicest clothes, print out your resume, and remind yourself to smile real big–and just when you think everything is going well, the interviewer hits you with a curveball question you aren't prepared for.

The best way for anything is to do your research ahead of time.

If you're preparing for a big interview, preparing beforehand with these 15 interview questions will help you get one step closer to that dream job.

Tell me about yourself?

Most interviews start with this question, and how you answer it will make your first impression. If you stumble over the answer and aren't quite sure what to say–

you're lack of confidence in yourself is showing.

If you start listing all your most significant accomplishments and talk too much, your ego might look a little too big. You need to find the right balance between being confident but not pretentious.

The best way to prepare for this question is to prepare an elevator pitch about who you are. Skip your personal history and give about 2-3 sentences about your career path and how you ended up in this interview, applying for this job.

You don't need to be too detailed; there are plenty of more questions coming. You want to leave enough curiosity that the interview becomes excited to learn more about you throughout the interview.

Why do you want to work for [insert company name]?

When a hiring manager asks this question, not only does that want to know why you want to work for them, but they also want to see what you know about the company.

This question tests how well you know what the company does and how passionate you are about the work they do—so make sure you understand the company well and can speak truthfully about your desires to work there.

How did you hear about this job?

When asked this during an interview, don't just say you heard about the job on a website. This is your opportunity to go into more detail about why you love this company and what motivates you to want to work there.

Moreover, if you have a personal connection at the company, this would be a good time to mention their name!

Tell me about something on your resume

Everyone has something on their resume that they're proud of. Whether it's a skill or achievement you've listed or a specific place you worked at, considering answering this question with the most exciting thing on your resume.

Plus, don't just say something relevant to your most recent position—you're already going to be asked about that. Instead, think back to one of the older positions listed on your resume and talk about how that job helped you grow into the person you are today.

Why are you looking for a job? Or why are you looking for a different job?

This question might seem innocuous, but this is how interviewers weed out the people who are either a) just looking for any job b) were fired from their last position or c) might have a high turnover rate, meaning you won't be sticking around for too long.

Focus on the positives and be specific. Think about why you are looking for a job: did you graduate, and this will be your first real job? Are you switching career paths? Are you leaving a current job for this one?

If you are currently working somewhere, you should also be prepared to answer, "why do you want to leave your current job for this one?"

Why should we hire you?

When asked this question, keep in mind that the recruiter is looking to hear what skills you have that you're going to bring to the team. Don't give a vague answer, such as, "I'm friendly and a hard worker." Instead, be specific, summarize your work history and achievements, and use numbers when possible.

In the example, say how many years of experience you have or name some of the accomplishments you made at your last company. The more specific you can be about what your skills are and how valuable of an employee you are, the better the interviewer will be able to picture you working there.

Where do you see yourself in five years?

This can seem like a big question during an interview, especially when you haven't prepared for it ahead of time. Keep in mind that you're in an interview setting—so you don't need to go into all the details about what your personal life goals are for the next five years. Focus on your career goals and be realistic.

If you plan to work at this company for five years, make sure you understand who would be working above you and what potential career growth there is. The hiring manager asks these questions to find out if you set realistic goals, if you are ambitious, and to confirm that the position you are interviewing for aligns with these goals and growth.

If this position isn't exactly a job with a lot of future opportunities, you can answer this by noting that you are not sure what your future is going to look like, but that you believe this position is going to help you navigate yourself in the right direction.

Tell me about a conflict you faced at work and how you dealt with it

This question is essential to ace because it helps an interviewer understand how you deal with conflict. It also helps test how well you think on your feet—so if you prepare ahead of time with a specific example, you'll avoid the awkward moment of silence while you try to think of a case.

Once you have an example in mind, explain what happened, how you professionally resolved the issue, and try to end the story with a happy note about how you reached a resolution or compromise with your co-worker.

What is your dream job?

Similar to the "where do you see yourself in five years" question, the interviewer is looking to understand how realistic you are when setting goals, how ambitious you are, and whether or not the job and company will be the right place for you to grow.

Again, try to set aside your personal goals (don't say your dream job is to be paid to take Instagram photos) and focus on your career goals. Think about how this job is going to set you up for the future and get you closer to your dream job. But, don't be that person who says, "to be CEO of this company."

What do you expect out of your team/co-workers?

This question is meant to understand how you work on a team and whether you will be the right cultural fit for the company. To prepare for this answer, make sure you research the company ahead of time.

You can always tell a little bit about what a company's culture is like by looking through their social media profiles or reading their reviews on Glassdoor.

What do you expect from your manager?

Again, the hiring manager is looking to understand what kind of employee you would be and whether you will be a good fit to add to their team. In some interviews, your future manager might be interviewing you. Answer this question as honestly as possible and pull examples from your current manager if you can show how they positively help you work better.

How do you deal with stress?

Answering this question will help hiring managers identify any potential red flags you might have. You want to show that you can handle stress professionally and positively that helps you continue working or won't stop you from accomplishing your goals.

Moreover, be specific and explain what you do to deal with stress—like taking a 15-minute break to take a walk outside, or crossing items off on a to-do list, etc.

What would the first 30 days in this position look like for you?

This question helps a company understand what you will get done in your first month, to three months in the position—and how you answer it will signal whether or not you're the right person for the job. Start by mentioning what information you would need to get started and what would help you transition into the new role. Then focus on your best skills and how you would apply those to this position right away.

What are your salary requirements?

Some interviewers ask this question; others don't. It's always better to be prepared, mainly because you want to make sure you would be paid a fair wage for the value you are going to add. That's why we built our Know Your Worth tool—to help you determine what you should be paid.

Do you have any questions?

The last question you will always be asked during an interview is whether or not you have any questions for the interviewer. This is your chance to stand out—so don't blow it by saying you don't, or that your questions have already been answered. Even if you don't have any questions—there's always a question you can ask at the end of an interview.

Keep a list of at least three to five questions in the back of your mind so that no matter what, there are at least two questions you have to ask at the end of the interview. Recruiters say that they enjoy getting to answer some questions at the end of a conversation—they did listen to you talk about themselves, so ask about them for a change.

Chapter 23: Make A Great First Impression

As mentioned once already in the early stage of this eBook a lot of people say and believe that: **There is no second chance to make a first impression.**

Unless you have an ace card hidden under your sleeve or a plan already worked out in order to look more professional than the other candidates and create an amazing first impression then you should strictly follow the below points.

In order to make the best possible first impression you should act like your interview has already began by the time you leave your house and you are on the way to your interview. Once you have arrived near the company space or company area that means that you will start interacting and see people from the company's environment. You may run into the CEO or CFO of the company in the parking area without even knowing it. Therefore it is extremely important that you act and treat everyone as professional as possible from the point that you leave your house to get to the place where the interview will take place.

Once I was told about an incident which a good friend of mine experienced. This person who is an HR Manager in an offshore company in Eastern Europe was on the way back to his company office after lunch break and while driving nearby the company office was cut off by a passing car. My friend used the horn of his car to notify the other car that he was there and the other person got out of his window and started calling him a variety of not polite names accompanied with bad gestures. My friend the HR Manager just decided to ignore this person and let him be and go on his way.

About 20 minutes later and once back to his office his secretary called him and advised that his 3 o'clock interview appointment was there. When the candidate walked into his office guess who was that person? Yes you have guessed it right! The candidate for the job opening and the crazy driver was one and the same person. The candidate though had absolutely no idea that the HR manager was the person that he was earlier shouting at the street. So the HR Manager decided to let the interview take place normally.

Everything took place and towards the end of the interview the HR Manager asked the candidate: "How well can you work under pressure and how do you manage stress?" The candidate's answer was: " Actually am really glad that you are making this question as i believe that this is an area where am proud of and one of my strongest strengths as a person is that I can handle stress really well and in general I am very calm as a person." Immediately after the candidate's answer the HR Manager announced to the candidate that the interview was completed and that due to the incident that took place earlier the day he had rejected the candidate.

This is a very good example of why we should always act and be as professional as possible.

Other points that you should take in serious consideration and follow in order to help you create an impressive first impression are the below.

Arrive for the interview about 15 to 20 minutes earlier than the actual scheduled appointment and attend the appointment alone. If you are escorted by a parent or a friend that sends a message that you cannot handle new tasks and experiences in your life without support. Before you enter the building where the interview will take place make sure that you switch your mobile phone on silent mode so that it won't disturb you or the interviewer on the duration of the interview.

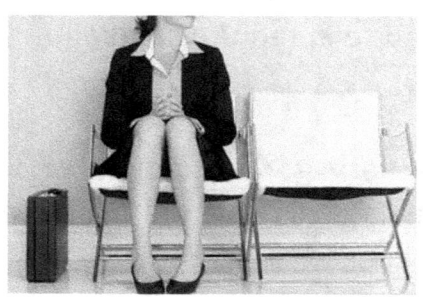

At no point you should chew gum while waiting to be called for the interview or during the interview. You could have a gum while driving towards the meeting location to refresh your breath but make sure you put it away once arrive in the location. Once you have entered the building you should be kind to the receptionist and anyone else you might meet. You do not know what kind of power and influence these people may have on the company's infrastructure.

If you are offered something to drink is better if you kindly declined the offer. Sit on the chair on the waiting area you have been advised and relax while waiting.

Make sure you sit up straight and take deep breaths occasionally as that helps the body and mind to relax.

Chapter 24: Covering Letter

When applying for a job vacancy, don't forget to accompany your CV with a covering letter. It is believed, a well written covering letter increases your chances of being called for interview but ensure that the letter is not a replica of your CV. [I have seen many recruiters in India skipping crafted letter after reading the subject and nothing beyond. See to that it is not a full length essay that would test patience to read]. **Covering letter** is British English and **Cover letter** is American.

Some tips on writing a good covering letter:

Some candidates use a generic covering letter for all jobs. It is necessary to modify it according to the job requirement.

If the recruiter's name is known, address it in the covering letter or address it to the Hiring Manager.

Clearly mention the subject of the covering letter. For e.g. Application for the position of Sales Manager (Ref: Times).

Give a brief introduction about yourself and the reference to the job notification to which you are responding.

In the next paragraph mention your suitability for the job. You take points from the job profile and write.

End the body of letter with a courteous note and ask them to feel free to let you know if they need any further information.

If you don't hear from them in 10 days, follow up. This shows your seriousness in the job opening. At the same time, it is impossible to track all those applied via portals for a follow up.

Dos of writing a covering letter

- Keep it short and simple
- Address the letter to a person or advertiser. If not mentioned then address it to 'Dear Madam /Sir'
- Customize your covering letter for different job positions
- Try to be assertive and polite
- Check the spellings and the grammar correct
- Hint on that you are eager to meet

Don'ts of writing a covering letter

- Repeating many 'I', 'my' in the letter shows your ego
- Using aggressive language
- Committing spelling mistakes
- Addressing yourself as Mr. / Ms.
- Sending out hand written covering letters

Letter writing rule says that when a letter is addressed to Dear ABC, it should end with 'Yours sincerely'. An apostrophe is not added in Yours. If addressed to Dear Sir, it should end with 'Yours faithfully'. It is becoming common to use 'Regards' irrespective of the nature of letter but I go with rule.

I have seen many candidates copying some phrases of the last century and applying it. Perhaps they would have taken it from essay writing books or old templates available on internet. Sometimes the vocabulary used has no relevancy to the competency standard exhibited by candidate.

Next time when you draft your covering letter, keep the all above points in mind. The chances of your CV getting short listed for an interview are bright.

Sample Covering Letter

<Today's Date>

From

<Your name>

<Your address>

<City name>< PIN>

To

The Director

PQR Technologies Ltd.,

<Address>

<City name><PIN>

Dear Sir,

Sub: Application for the position of Software Engineer

This is with reference to your advertisement in the <newspaper/Job portal> dated<date> for Software Engineer position. I would like to formally submit my resume for consideration.

With 2 years experience in software engineering, possess skills in Visual Basic, Java and .NET development, C development. I have proficiency in website design, HTML, CSS and JavaScript. Currently I am a Software Programmer at JJJ Infotech.

I look forward to a personal interview at your convenience.

Thanking you,

Yours faithfully,

<Your signature>

Chapter 25: Nuances Of Effective Communication Skills

What's the right way to introduce yourself to a job interview? How can you continue an interview to make the best impression possible?

Next, experiences will play a major role in how an applicant views you as a nominee. Anything you say in the first step of the interview can make a big difference in the result—in a good way or in a bad way. You don't want to come across as awkward and lacking social skills. Instead, if you were to be hired, you'll want to show that you have the professionalism and communication skills to succeed in a new job.

Many hiring managers may even make a decision to deny an applicant on the grounds of what they did not do when they met. Of example, whether you happen to be late or check your mobile regularly, you're going to want to curtail those patterns before you get a job interview.

The hiring manager may see the actions as an inability to make a promise and follow-up—not the characteristics that will be precious to the prospective employer. Small details make a big difference at this point in the search for a job. That's why it's important to pay attention to the way you talk and think carefully about how you're going to present yourself during a job interview.

Don't Let Language Be a Threat to Your Career Success Interviews are exhausting enough without the extra pressure of having to make sure you use the correct pronunciation, voice, syntax and formalities of the English spoken language. If you're actually from a different culture or history in an English-speaking country struggling for your rightful place on the corporate ladder, but without much traction, then you're not lonely.

You may have been eligible to get an interview because of your application, which shows your strengths and skills and qualifications. The boss loves it and asks you to an appointment to find out more about it. The only difficulty is that he or she does not understand you and assumes that you do not have a strong command of the English language and therefore do not fulfill one of the essential requirements of the position of the job-good communication skills.

I have interacted with many people who have come to me because of their inability to articulate their skills and attributes successfully and honestly. Time and time again, because of their language skills, they have lost opportunities, and many of them eventually give up hope and agree that they should not even try to advance within their companies or choose a career path. It was Nelson Mandela who said, "There is no passion to be found to play small-to settle for a life that is less than the life that you are capable of living." Talk about what's feasible and concentrate on it - there's always a path, and there's always someone who can support.

The techniques that I use for my clients to strengthen their interaction so that they can succeed effectively and have a lot to do with confidence on a more even basis. When a person is nervous, it is more difficult to think clearly and to convey a message. The first thing you need to do is try and understand your anxiety or nervousness.

Applicants for whom English has never been their first language will become different when they have to communicate in English, particularly in a test circumstance such as an interview. We lose their confidence, question their ability, and try to avoid too much interaction in the expectation that they will be mocked or forced to repeat themselves over and over again. Sadly, there are many idle listeners in the world today. Everyone is in a hurry, and they don't want to waste their time trying to understand or get to know someone with a dialect that distracts from what they're trying to say. We have to presume that the question is the same individual. He or she may have a dozen or more candidates to interview in a week, and they don't want to work to understand what the applicant is saying.

Conclusion

With the information you have right now, you should be more than able to handle any job interview. These encounters will start to get easier the more you prepare and your chances of getting the job goes up.

One thing you have to remember, though, is that there will always be a chance that you won't make the cut. This could be by no fault of yours. There could just be a better candidate or a management policy. Never take it too hard. Although a failure means you didn't make it, that doesn't mean you're not worth the time and effort.

On the plus side, there will always be jobs available to you as long as you keep looking and preparing well. Remember the first few lessons in this book that talked about preparation. As long as you develop the habit of doing your homework and coming prepared for an interview, you will always have high chances of landing that job.

At this point, you should already be more than ready for your next interview. Keep in mind the necessity to give off a great first impression by smiling, giving a great handshake and sitting firmly at the edge of your seat.

Finally, remember to treat the interview as a formal conversation. With that being said, do not sit and just wait for the interviewer to ask you questions. It is not an interrogation. Do not be afraid to speak up especially when something they say catches your interest. Interviewers are people, too. You can ask them questions about the company and their policies when the need arises. Asking questions shows interviewers that you were paying attention to them and you want to make sure that you understand them well.

With that being said, go break a leg!

www.ingramcontent.com/pod-product-compliance
Lightning Source LLC
Chambersburg PA
CBHW072003070526
44583CB00015B/1314